SAILORS OF 1812

Memoirs and Letters of Naval Officers on Lake Ontario

by
James Richardson
Arthus Sinclair
Henry Kent
and
Barzallai Pease

• • • • • • • •

Edited,
with an
Introduction and Notes
by
Robert Malcomson

• • • • • • • •

Illustrated
by
George Balbar

• • • • • • • •

©1997
OLD FORT NIAGARA ASSOCIATION, INC,
YOUNGSTOWN, NEW YORK

ISBN: 0-941967-19-0

For

Janet, Carrie and Melanie

hic et ubique

Table of Contents

    page

Acknowledgements 4

Introduction: Naval Service on Lake Ontario, 1812-1815 5

Editor's Note 18

Part I - The Memoirs of James Richardson, PM, 1812-13 21
    1. Service with the Provincial Marine 22
    2. John Dennis, the Ship Builder 26
    3. The Attack on Sackets Harbor, 29 May 1813 28
    4. Raiding the American Shore 31
    5. The Failed Cutting-Out Expedition 34

Part II - The Correspondence of Arthur Sinclair, USN 39
    1. To John Cocke, 4 July 1813 39
    2. To John Cocke, 25 August 1813 48
    3. To William Jones, 22 August 1813 53
    4. From William Jones, 16 September 1813 55
    5. To John Cocke, 10 October 1813 56
    6. To John Cocke, 30 November 1813 64

Part III - The Narrative of Henry Kent, RN 73
    1. Setting Out on the Journey 73
    2. Through the Wintry Drifts 75
    3. On to Quebec 78
    4. From Quebec to Kingston 79

Part IV - The Memoirs of James Richardson, RN, 1814-15 81
    1. The Attack on Oswego, 6 May 1814 81
    2. The Battle of Sandy Creek, 30 May 1814 83
    3. The Great Ships of Lake Ontario 85

Part V - The Journal of Barzallai Pease, US Army 91
    1. A Job in the Transport Service 91
    2. After the War 93

About the Editor 96

Acknowledgements

The editor and the Old Fort Niagara Association would like to express their gratitude to the following people and institutions that helped make this book possible.

The Special Collections Department of the University of Virginia Library granted permission to use the Sinclair letters, contained in the John Hartwell Cocke Papers (#642) held by that institution, and provided copies of the original correspondence. The Department of Special Collections of the Syracuse University Library willingly provided access to the Pease Journals and permission to use the material.

Among the people who assisted with related research or critiqued drafts of the manuscript were Donald E. Graves, Dennis Gannon, Thomas Malcomson, Carrie Malcomson, Patrick Wilder, Historic Site Manager, Fort Ontario State Historic Site and First President and Founder of the Sackets Harbor Historical Society, and Brian Dunnigan, formerly the Executive Director of the Old Fort Niagara Association.

Commodore Sir James Lucas YEO
Royal Navy

Introduction

Naval Service on Lake Ontario, 1812-1815

> "To Sackett's Harbor Yeo steered, with Prevost's chosen blood hounds,
> But Brown his dogs of valor cheered, militia blood, but good hounds,
> He chased them from the bloody track, and Yeo's bull-dogs slighting,
> Though Chauncey was not there, he show'd Sir James the art of fighting.
> Bow, wow, wow!
> Fresh-water dogs can tutor them with bow, wow, wow!"
> Old Song - *A New Bow Wow.*

"I want to take this gallant Knight. I will if I do so, *bring him to Virginia in a Cage and shew him as a curiosity.*" This is how Arthur Sinclair half-jokingly expressed his ardor to have at the squadron of Commodore Sir James Lucas Yeo and squash it. As he made his proclamation, Sinclair had yet to encounter the British and, much to his disappointment, when he did, his vivid dreams of glory were not realized. Sinclair's quest for victory was not totally in vain for he left behind a descriptive, personal account of his experiences during the War of 1812 on the Lake Ontario station in a series of letters to a friend in Virginia. The letters are presented in print for the first time in this volume.

Sinclair's letters are accompanied by the words of three of his contemporaries: James Richardson, Henry Kent and Barzallai Pease. Richardson began the war as a member of the Provincial Marine. His "Reminiscences" were printed in an obscure journal early in this century. Lieutenant Henry Kent of the Royal Navy wrote a letter home describing his remarkable journey to the lakes, which was published in England in 1815. Barzallai Pease recorded his brief term with the U. S. Army in one volume of the detailed journal he kept during his long career at sea. Like Sinclair's correspondence, the Pease excerpt has never been printed before.

Documentary evidence of the naval buildup and campaigns on Lake Ontario abounds, although thorough analyses of the evidence are rare.[1] Also lacking are personal accounts of events recorded by the men who sailed the

---

[1] Key works dealing with the war on Lake Ontario include: Theodore Roosevelt, *The Naval War of 1812* (New York, 1882; reprint: Annapolis, MD, 1987); A. T. Mahon, *Sea Power in Its Relations to the War of 1812*, 2 volumes (London, 1905); E. A Cruikshank, "The Contest for the Command of Lake Ontario in 1812 and 1813," *Transactions of the Royal Society of Canada*, 10 (1916), pp. 161-223; E. A. Cruikshank, "The Contest for the Command of Lake Ontario in 1814," *Ontario History*, 21 (1924), pp. 99-159; William Dudley (ed.), *The War of 1812: A Documentary History*, 2 volumes (Washington, 1985, 1992).

ships.[2] Ned Myers's days with Commodore Chauncey formed part of his life story, which was reprinted by the Naval Institute Press in 1989,[3] but no other recent publication has been devoted to the eyewitness accounts of participants in the war on Lake Ontario. This volume was conceived to fill that gap and to serve as a companion piece for Donald E. Graves's *Soldiers of 1814: American Enlisted Men's Memoirs of the Niagara Campaign.*[4]

When the War of 1812 began, only a handful of warships existed on Lake Ontario. The single American cruiser was the brig *Oneida*, launched at Oswego in 1809 for the express purpose of enforcing an embargo imposed by the government of President Thomas Jefferson. The *Oneida* was referred to as a brig because it had two masts upon which "square" sails were hung from thick spars at right angles to the vessel's midline. As with any square-rigged vessel, the *Oneida* also had "fore and aft" sails (or sails rigged along its midline), but it relied on its large spread of square canvas to harness the wind's power and propel its heavily burdened hull through the water. When fully equipped with ordnance, the brig carried sixteen 24-pounder carronades, chosen for their smaller size, but destructive fire power. Since carronades were only effective over a distance of about 500 yards, the *Oneida* was also given a 32-pounder long gun, mounted on a pivot in its bows, for use against targets at longer range. The weight of this latter gun was so great that the sailing qualities of the brig were affected detrimentally, so it was removed. When fully manned, the *Oneida* carried about 145 officers, men and marines.[5]

The *Oneida* was opposed by a Provincial Marine squadron. This force had evolved from the Royal Navy detachment that had served on the lake during the Seven Years War (1756-1763) and it was administered by the Quartermaster General's Department of the British Army at Quebec. The Provincial

---

[2] The National Archives of Canada (NAC) holds two manuscripts concerning men who served on Lake Ontario: "Four Years on the Lakes of Canada ..." by David Wingfield, NAC, Manuscript Group [MG] 24, F 18 (a portion of which was published in David Ellison, "David Wingfield and Sacketts Harbour", *Dalhousie Review*, 52 (1972), pp. 407-413); and a memorial biography of William Howe Mulcaster, NAC, MG 24, F 95. Excerpts from personal letters written by a third British officer were published in M. K. and C. Ritchie, "A Laker's Log," *The American Neptune*, 17 (1957), pp. 203-211. The letters are those of John Frederick Johnston, part of the Halsey Papers (ref. 16221-16356) held by the County Record Office of Hertford, Hertfordshire, U. K.

[3] J. Fenimore Cooper (ed.), *Ned Myers; or A Life Before the Mast* (Philadelphia, 1843; reprint: Annapolis, MD, 1989).

[4] Published by the Old Fort Niagara Association, Inc., Youngstown, NY, 1995.

[5] For an article about the *Oneida*, see Richard F. Palmer, "James Fenimore Cooper and the Navy Brig *Oneida*," *Inland Seas*, 40 (1984), pp. 90-99. The best source available for information on the warships of Lake Ontario is Howard I. Chapelle, *The History of The American Sailing Navy: The Ships and their Development* (New York, 1949).

Marine had always operated schooners on Lake Ontario, vessels with two masts rigged with large fore and aft sails. Occasionally square sails were added to the top portion of the fore- or mainmast, earning such a vessel the name of "topmast" schooner. A fore and aft rig was simpler than a square rig, and the Provincial Marine vessels were not always armed, so they carried relatively small crews. The vessels of the Marine Department, as it was also known, were generally used for transporting government officials, provisions and troops among the key ports.

Sharing the lake with the warships were just over two dozen commercial carriers. Most of them were schooners, built with large holds and shallow drafts so that they could pass over the bars that obstructed most bays. Some of these lakers were sloops, having one mast each and a fore and aft rig. In addition, commercial traffic was also carried by bateaux, rafts and other assorted watercraft.

In June 1812 the Provincial Marine squadron on Lake Ontario consisted of three vessels.[6] One, the schooner *Duke of Gloucester*, was in such bad repair that a new schooner, the *Prince Regent*, was being built at York to replace it. The other two vessels were "ships," that is, they were three-masted and square-rigged. The *Earl of Moira*, launched in 1805, was very small for such an arrangement and in 1813 it was re-rigged as a brig. The *Royal George*, launched in 1809, was large enough to be properly ship-rigged. It was fitted with a sufficient number of ports to house twenty guns on its spar deck (the flush, upper deck of the ship). The *Royal George* was commonly referred to as a corvette since it was a good deal smaller than a frigate, the handiest class of warship in navies of the period. During the War of 1812 three other corvettes, one at Kingston (the *Wolfe*) and two on Lake Erie (the *Queen Charlotte* and the *Detroit*), were built along the lines of the *Royal George*.

Schooners, brigs and corvettes were the main warships operated by the British and Americans on Lake Ontario in 1812 and 1813. For a brief period the American squadron consisted of two corvettes, one brig, and thirteen schooners. Most of the latter vessels were lakers that had been bought by the U. S. Navy and armed. They were frequently referred to by the Americans as gunboats. The British had gunboats also, but they were purposely built for restricted naval use on rivers and along the coasts.

---

[6] For more information about the British Lake Ontario squadron, see Richard Preston, "The Fate of Kingston's Warships," *Historic Kingston,* 1 (1974), pp. 3-14. Design, construction and armament specifics may be found in the following documents: "A Statement of Naval Forces on Lake Ontario" by Richard O'Conor, 14 October 1814, NAC, MG 12, Admiralty 106, vol. 1997, unpaginated; "A Statement of the Naval Force on Lake Onatrio, January 1815" by Robert Hall, *ibid.*; "Statement of the Naval Force on Lake Ontario, 1815" by Thomas Strickland, 10 June 1815, *ibid.*

At one time or another the naval vessels were collectively referred to as ships, but by the standards of strict navy vernacular, only the corvettes were truly "ships." Occasionally, the corvettes were also called "sloops," not to be confused with the single-masted commercial carriers. This category was applied when a warship was captained by a "commander" in the Royal Navy or a "master commandant" in the U. S. Navy. In fact, if an officer with such a rank was given charge of a brig, its official status changed to "sloop."

Frigates first appeared on Lake Ontario in the spring of 1814. They were three-masted and square-rigged, and their main gundecks were below their upper decks so that they could carry upwards of 40 guns. A frigate usually had an open waist in the middle portion of its upper deck, but on Lake Ontario the waist was closed in on some ships so that more guns could be mounted after the style of the heavy American frigates like the United States Ship *Constitution*. The frigates were massive vessels, crewed by hundreds of men and possessing enormous fire power. One of them, the USS *Superior*, was arguably the strongest American ship launched before 1815.

The grandest of all the Lake Ontario warships was His Majesty's Ship *St. Lawrence*, launched in September 1814. It carried over one hundred guns on three decks and required a crew of more than six hundred. By most contemporary standards, it was a match for the "first rate," line-of-battle ships that plied the oceans. Had the war extended into 1815, four more first-rates would have been launched on Lake Ontario, all of them bigger than the *St. Lawrence*.

A couple of hundred men started the naval war on Lake Ontario, but in time they were joined by thousands. The Americans travelled north from New York City and west along the Mohawk River. Some ventured on by water to Oswego while others went overland from Rome or Utica to Sackets Harbor. The British all passed through Quebec and up the St. Lawrence to Kingston. As the size of each squadron increased, so did the need to operate the warships more effectively. This responsibility rested squarely on the shoulders of the naval officers. Although the navies differed from one another, the job was the same; the men who walked the quarterdeck made the decisions that saved or lost the day.

The ranks used by the Provincial Marine and the United States Navy were based on the system established by the Royal Navy.[7] There were four general categories of men in the British navy. In ascending order, they were: seamen, petty officers, warrant officers and commissioned officers. Petty officers (boatswain's mates, quartermasters, etc.) were drawn from the population of seamen and given warrants, or certificates, by the Navy Board (an arm of the

---

[7] For a full discussion of the officers of the Royal Navy, see Brian Lavery, *Nelson's Navy: The Ships, Men and Organization, 1793-1815* (London, 1989).

British Admiralty in London) to perform their duties as long as they met their captains' standards. Warrant officers also received their warrants from the Navy Board and while some of them shared the same status aboard ship as petty officers, others enjoyed accomodations aft and were permitted to walk the quarterdeck, territory normally reserved for commissioned officers. Among the highest ranking warrant officers was the master, whose navigational skills and wide knowledge of routes and currents, shoals and shores made him indispensable to the captain.

The "captain" of a ship was always a commissioned officer, that is, one who had been awarded a commission by the Lords of the Admiralty who sat on the Admiralty Board. A commissioned officer could aspire to attain "flag" rank and command a fleet of warships, whereas a warrant officer rarely had influence beyond his own vessel. The route to a captaincy was a long and difficult one. Unlike military service, advancement through the ranks of the Royal Navy did not require the purchase of commissions, although patronage, or "interest" as it was known, was an important asset in a young man's rise in both services. Almost invariably a career began when the son of an aristocrat, a professional man or a naval officer, who had passed his eleventh birthday, was appointed a "Volunteer Class I" aboard one of His Majesty's Ships. By the regulations of 1794 the candidate could be appointed to the rank of midshipman after three years of service. Abuse of this system was not unknown, and more than a few boys earned their three-year credits without ever being afloat, and before they were eleven years of age.

The rank of midshipman was only an appointment, but it gave a young man the opportunity to develop the many different skills involved in handling ships, boats, ordnance and men. When he had accrued six years of experience after the date of his name first being entered on a ship's muster, and he was nineteen years old, a midshipman could take the lieutenant's examination. By that time he might have been advanced to the rank of master's mate, which indicated that he was sharing increased responsibilities in his ship and was ready for promotion. He might even have been made an "acting" lieutenant to fill a vacancy. The majority of acting positions were confirmed by the Admiralty after the officer had passed his oral exam before a board of captains, and he was given a commission as a lieutenant. He then spent several years or longer at sea until he was able to advance to the post of first lieutenant, executive officer to the captain. In 1812 there were more than 3,000 lieutenants in the Royal Navy.

The British naval officer's next step was to rise beyond the role of subordinate and attain his own vessel. There were no further formal examinations of skill and aptitude to identify promising candidates. Patronage helped some men, while others caught the eye of a flag officer at the right place and time, and others distinguished themselves in combat. A lucky officer might become a "lieutenant commander" of a schooner or a brig, but the preferred path was to be promoted to the rank of "commander," (known, prior to the 1790s, as "master and commander"). Once advanced to this rank, the officer received a commission for a vessel that usually carried between ten and eighteen guns and was referred to as a "sloop," no matter what kind of rig it had. In 1812 there were 586 commanders in the Royal Navy, but only 168 vessels suitable for them to command, so many promising, young men were frustrated in their desire for promotion. Robert Heriot Barclay, who eventually lost the British squadron to Oliver Hazard Perry on Lake Erie in 1813, was considered ready for promotion for four years before he was finally advanced to acting-commander (later confirmed) and sent to the lakes.

While the courtesy title of "captain" was applied to any man who commanded a vessel, advancement to a formal captaincy only occurred when an officer was assigned to a "sixth rate"ship, one bearing twenty to thirty guns guns. Such a vessel was considered a "post" ship because its commanding officer's name was posted on the Admiralty's seniority list of captains. If the man survived long enough, his name would ascend the list and he would eventually attain the rank of admiral. Along the way he might be given supervision of a squadron of vessels, for which additional responsibility he held the temporary title, rather than rank, of commodore. Sir James Lucas Yeo reached this level of achievement in 1813, but did not live long enough to become an admiral.

As it evolved during the latter half of the 18th century, the Provincial Marine adapted many of the Royal Navy traditions. Due to its small size, few officers were needed.[8] In 1811 on Lake Ontario there was only one master and commander (the old term was still used on the lakes), and four lieutenants, two of whom commanded vessels. The senior officer was referred to as "commodore," but his responsibilities were minimal compared to the role of a Royal Navy commodore. Only in 1812 was it recommended that each commanding officer be required to appoint a single young man to the rank of midshipman so that he might be trained properly over a period of three or four years.[9]

The Provincial Marine proved to be unequal to the task posed by war conditions.[10] In October 1812 the governor-in-chief and commander of the

---

[8] "Proposed Establishment of the Provincial Marine ...," 30 August 1811, NAC, RG 8, I, "C series," vol. 728, p. 60.

[9] "Report upon the Provincial Marine ...," 24 February 1812, *ibid.*, pp. 86-93.

[10] For an assessment of the Provincial Marine, see W. A. B. Douglas, "The Anatomy of Naval Incompetence: The Provincial Marine in Defence of Upper Canada before 1813," *Ontario History*, 71 (1979), pp. 3-25.

British forces in British North America, Lieutenant General Sir George Prevost, complained to his superiors in Britain that its "officers are in general deficient in experience and particularly in that energetic spirit which distinguishes British seamen."[11] The British government responded by sending a detachment of more than 450 officers and seamen of the Royal Navy under the command of Commodore Yeo, and a second smaller group from Bermuda under Barclay, to the lakes to take over from the Provincial Marine. All the officers in the Marine Department were encouraged to continue serving, but most of them were so insulted by being superseded by the Royal Navy officers that they quit. Those who remained kept their wages, but operated in positions of reduced authority.

When the United States Navy was founded in 1794 the system for manning its ships was based loosely on the Royal Navy model. Naval men, revolutionary war veterans, government officials and high ranking families used their influence to have their sons admitted to the service, generally, in their mid-teens. Their appointments were formalized by the issuance of warrants from the secretary of the navy and the pledges of allegiance before judges. Examinations were used temporarily around 1803 to select qualified midshipmen for promotion, but they were dropped in favour of a selection-by-merit approach. In the words of Secretary of the Navy William Jones, "If you have conceived the idea of *rank* among *midshipmen*, you are mistaken....They are all novitiates, and the rule is to promote them according to their several merits, acquirements, and services."[12]

There was a second route, albeit a limited one, by which command of a small American war vessel could be attained. As in the Royal Navy, the navigation expert aboard a warship was a warrant officer, holding the rank of "sailing master" in the U.S. Navy. His subordinates, or understudies, were "master's mates," not to be confused with the Royal Navy master's mates, who were advanced midshipmen. When an American master's mate was advanced to sailing master, he might expect to begin his duties in command of a gunboat. Sometimes, an experienced commercial seaman would be taken into the U.S. Navy as a sailing master. Advancement to a larger command or to the rank of lieutenant was rare. The Lake Ontario lakers that were converted into gunboats were frequently commanded by sailing masters.

Promotion beyond lieutenancy in the American navy was based on performance, although the influence of patronage was never absent. Some

---

[11] Prevost to Earl Bathurst, 17 October 1812, NAC, MG 11, Colonial Office 42, vol. 147, p. 215.

[12] Cited in Christopher McKee, *A Gentlemanly and Honorable Profession: The Creation of the U. S. Naval Officer Corps, 1794-1815* (Annapolis, MD, 1991), p. 277. Description of the American system is based on material in McKee's book.

officers held strong views on the matter of seniority, believing that it should be the key criterion in determining advancement, but their arguments achieved little. As the need arose, the Navy Department selected men for promotion to the rank of "master commandant," similar to the British "commander," and then on to a full captaincy. While dates of first commissions in each rank were carefully recorded, seniority did not mean as much in the U. S. Navy as it did in the Royal Navy. Although the Americans officers still referred to themselves as "post captains," there was no need for a seniority list because there were no admirals in the American service until the Civil War. Any one of the captains might be called upon to act as a commodore for a period of time.

The U.S. Navy was very much smaller than the Royal Navy. In 1812, while more than 3,000 Royal Navy lieutenants and 586 commanders hoped for promotion, there were only 70 lieutenants and 9 masters commandant in the American service. Because the American system of promotion was less steeped in tradition, it was subject to debate and controversy. When, for instance, Charles Morris was promoted from lieutenant directly to captain because of the part he played as first lieutenant aboard the USS *Constitution* when it conquered HMS *Guerriere* in August 1812, other officers protested. One of the critics was Arthur Sinclair, then a master commandant, who expressed the view, shared by others, that it was inappropriate for Morris to surpass seven more experienced lieutenants and eight masters commandant.[13] As shown in Part II, Sinclair was involved in another promotion-related problem in 1813 when he was advanced to captain while still commanding a diminutive corvette on an unpleasant station and sharing the quarterdeck with Commodore Isaac Chauncey.

A service afloat that was much smaller than even the U.S. Navy was the transport arm of the U.S. Army. This was a collection of vessels employed in carrying men and materiel among army posts. The army had maintained vessels on Lake Erie after 1802, and other boats and small schooners were operated on Lake Ontario during the war because Barzallai Pease was hired to supervise the "squadron" at Sackets Harbor.[14]

Having covered some of the background information needed to appreciate the words of the War of 1812 veterans, it is time to learn something about each of the men whose writings are featured here.

---

[13] Described in *ibid.*, pp. 299-300. See also, Sinclair to Jones, 28 March 1813, United States National Archives (USNA), RG 45, "Letters Received by the Secretary of the Navy from Commanders, 1804-1886," Microcopy 147, Reel 5, item 39.

[14] For more information about the history of the army transport service, see Charles D. Gibson and E. Kay Gibson, *Marine Transportation in War: The U. S. Army Experience 1775-1860*, vol. 1, *The Army's Navy* Series, (Camden, ME, 1992). This volume makes no mention of the service on Lake Ontario.

James Richardson (1791-1875) left a narrative that covers the full length of the war, from his service with the Provincial Marine through his actions alongside Commodore Yeo.[15] He was a lieutenant in the Marine when Yeo arrived but, unlike most of his officer-colleagues, he did not quit. He lost his lieutenancy, but kept his rate of pay and the right to be a member of the wardroom mess because he agreed to act as a pilot owing to his knowledge of local navigation. Although the record is unclear, Richardson appears to have been given a Royal Navy master's warrant in 1814.

The origin of his "Reminiscences" is uncertain, but it seems likely that they were put together from a number of lectures that Richardson gave long after the war had ended when he had gained some social status as a Methodist minister. The original memoir was a rambling and convoluted piece that confused events and chronology. To make it easier to comprehend, it has been abridged to eliminate repetitious or irrelevant paragraphs to put the events in proper sequence.

Richardson's memoir is a significant addition to the study of the War of 1812 on Lake Ontario, as no previous historians appear to have used it as a source. It has special value since it is the only known personal narrative attributable to a member of the Provincial Marine during the war. Although his adventures were recalled from the distance of later life, Richardson's accounts are dependable when compared to other reports. Nothing he said about the critical encounters between the squadrons during the second half of 1813 was recorded, but his descriptions of other attacks, raids and manoeuvres provide valuable information and insight. In order to create a smooth chronology for this volume, the memoir has been split into two sections, the first dealing with the years 1812-13 and the second with 1814-15.

What kind of man was James Richardson? The memoir reveals a person who bore no grudges for the upsets and hardships he experienced and there are no harsh or critical words for his superiors or wardroom companions. His post war career as a minister, and eventually a bishop, may have moderated some youthful opinions, but there is evidence that he was always an unpretentious man and a hard worker. As proof of his selfless devotion to duty, there is the assertion that he did not notice that an American round shot had sheared off his left arm, at Oswego in May 1814, until he reached for something and discovered he lacked the hand to do the grasping.

---

[15] James Richardson, "Incidents in the Early History of the Settlements in the Vicinity of Lake Ontario: Reminiscences of Lieut. James Richardson: later the Rev. James Richardson, D. D., Bishop of the M. E. Church," *Annual Report and Transactions of the Women's Canadian Historical Society of Toronto*, #15 (Toronto, 1915-16). An article about Richardson may be found in F. G. Halpenny (ed.), *Dictionary of Canadian Biography* (Toronto, 1983) (hereafter: *DCB*), vol. 10, pp. 615-7.

Arthur Sinclair (ca. 1780-1831) was no less dedicated than James Richardson, but more concerned about rank, respect and glory. Sinclair was a fifteen-year veteran of the U. S. Navy when he was assigned to Commodore Isaac Chauncey's squadron in 1813. Ranked as a master commandant, he was expecting to assume independent command of Chauncey's new corvette, the *General Pike*, but was disappointed when the commodore hoisted his flag on the ship and made most of the critical decisions about its deployment. The situation became unbearable after Sinclair was promoted to a full captaincy in July, and he protested, gently, to Secretary of the Navy William Jones. Actually, Sinclair made complaints about all sorts of things: the weather, the soldiers he had to transport, his fellow officers, the unappreciative public and the campaign goals chosen by the generals. Simply put, he hated the Lake Ontario service and could hardly wait to escape it.

There is no biography of Arthur Sinclair, so information about him must be gleaned from a number of sources.[16] He was most certainly still in his teens when he joined the U. S. Navy in 1798 as a midshipman. He enjoyed the enviable distinction of serving aboard the USS *Constellation* in 1799 when it fought the French frigate *L'Insurgente* and earned the Navy's first official victory. Like many of his contemporaries, Sinclair saw action in the Tripolitan War and then returned home to the gunboat service. He was promoted to lieutenant in 1804 and master commandant in 1812. Prior to being sent to Lake Ontario, Arthur Sinclair commanded the schooner *Enterprise* and the brigs, *Nautilus* and *Argus*. He was in charge of the gunboats on the Potomac River during the spring of 1813 when he was ordered to Lake Ontario, from which he gained a leave in December to recover from an illness. In 1814 Sinclair returned to the lakes as commodore of the squadron on the upper lakes stationed at Erie, Pennsylvania, where he pursued an active but mainly unsuccessful campaign. Any command afloat that he had following the war was brief, for it appears that he spent the balance of his career in command of the naval station at Norfolk, Virginia. He died there on 7 February 1831.

A portrait of Arthur Sinclair, said to have been painted in 1813, was used for his depiction in this volume, but an equally graphic portrayal of the man came from the pen of his second wife, Sarah "Sally" Skipwith (Kennon) Sinclair. After announcing her engagement to a friend, Miss Kennon offered the following description of her fiancé:

---

[16] Personal and professional information is found in the Kennon Letters, published in 26 separate installments in *The Virginia Magazine of History and Biography*, 30- 40 (1922-1932). Incidents in Sinclair's career are described in McKee, *A Gentlemanly and Honorable Profession*. Other professional information may be found among naval records in U. S. Congress, *American State Papers: Naval Affairs, Vol. 1*, (Washington, 1832-61).

> he is neither tall nor short; but just the middle size; his form and appearance is very elegant; . . . his skin is naturally very fair; but being exposed so constantly to the sun, all his visible parts are very much tanned; how his invisibles are I am unable to tell you; he is neither fat or lean but just what you may call plump; but oh lord . . . Ellen I must tell you the truth, as I am upon honour; he is quite Ugly. . . . he has an ugly nose, not pretty eyes and white eye brows and white eye lashes; but then he has a very sweet looking mouth, and that is a very great thing in a matrimonial voyage.[17]

The voyage proved to be a successful one. The Sinclairs had four daughters and four sons, three of whom served in the navies of the United States and the Confederate States.

The four private letters printed here were sent by Sinclair to his friend, John Hartwell Cocke, the brother of Sinclair's first wife who had died along with their twin children by 1803.[18] The two other letters were exchanges between Sinclair and the secretary of the navy. Previously unpublished, they offer the viewpoints of a man who typified naval officers of the period. He lusted for victory over the enemy and all its attendant glory and he was quickly irritated by the failure to achieve his goals and not hesitant about plainly expressing his frustrations. At the same time, he admired the natural beauty of the Lake Ontario region and considered buying land there. He was always concerned about his family and very much missed his new wife and the two children she had already borne him. And, of course, he was a thorough seaman, much enamoured of his ships, and completely competent in handling them in any conditions. During the "Burlington Races" in September 1813, Sinclair was ready to sail the *Pike* right into the British anchorage, regardless of the hazardous weather and enemy batteries. One almost believes that if Chauncey had let Sinclair have his way, Perry's Lake Erie victory might have been paralleled on Ontario and Sinclair would have won his laurels.[19]

The date of Henry Kent's birth is unknown, but it seems likely that he had barely reached his eleventh birthday by 1800 when he joined the Royal Navy as a first class volunteer aboard a prison ship, HMS *Fortitude*, at Portsmouth,

---

[17] S. Kennon to E. Mordecai, 2 August 1809, "Kennon Letters," *The Virginia Magazine of History and Biography*, 32 (1924), p. 79.

[18] The letters printed here are from the John Hartwell Cocke Papers (#642), Special Collections Department, University of Virginia Library.

[19] Sinclair was presented with a sword by the State of Virginia for his actions during the "Burlington Races."

England.[20] He came from a family of Royal Navy officers, and one of them probably arranged for his name to be put on the books of the *Fortitude*. In 1803 he was transferred to another ship and given the rank of midshipman. Kent passed through seven ships between 1803 and March 1811 when he was promoted to lieutenant aboard HM Sloop *Fantome*. In that vessel he saw action in the North Sea and along the Spanish coast and across the Atlantic in raids against the Americans around Chesapeake Bay.

In the winter of 1813-14 Kent volunteered to join a Royal Navy detachment of 210 officers and men leaving Halifax to trek overland to Kingston. Under the command of Commander Edward Collier, that detachment sailed to Saint John, New Brunswick, from where the men undertook their 900-mile march to Lake Ontario. For the Royal Navy it was an unprecedented endeavour, especially since Collier, Kent and the others made the trip through the dead of Canadian winter. They left Saint John on 26 January 1814 and arrived at Kingston on 22 March, having lost only one man to the cold.

Henry Kent described the expedition in a letter to his father, which was published in *The Naval Chronicle* in 1815.[21] It is clear that conditions on the journey challenged Kent's fortitude, but his recollection of the trip is devoid of grumbling. Even in one of the darkest hours when men in his division lay down in a blizzard and refused to go further, Kent recalled, "I endeavoured by every persuasion to cheer them, and succeeded in getting about one half to accompany me." Stiff upper lip, indeed!

A ship's company in snowshoes trudging over snow drifts is an incongruous image, but, in the context of the Lake Ontario campaign, it made sense. With the squadrons expanding, more men were needed, so the duty-bound seamen walked to war. Kent tells the story without much ado, as if the trek was something that any officer worth his salt could be expected to do at the turn of the watch glass. Competently and almost routinely, Henry Kent marshalled his men and pressed them on from post to post until they reached Kingston and joined their ships.

Henry Kent was rewarded for his troubles by being made first lieutenant of one of the new ships under construction at Kingston. He remained with the squadron until the war ended and then was sent to the upper lakes where he sailed among the Royal Navy establishments until 1819. After a three year stint on Lake Champlain, he finally returned to England and gained promotion to commander. In 1825 he entered semi-retirement as a half-pay officer and

---

[20] For a biographical sketch of Kent, see William O'Byrne (ed.), *A Naval Biographical Dictionary...*(London, 1849), p. 608.

[21] "Extraordinary March of Lieutenant Henry Kent..." *The Naval Chronicle*, 33 (1815), pp. 123-7.

maintained that status through the rest of his life, which extended past 1849.

Barzallai Pease (1773-?) is the author of the fourth narrative. He differs from his contemporaries in a number of ways. Most pertinently, he was not a member of any navy. He went to sea at the age of sixteen in 1789 aboard a whaling ship and between then and 1814 he cruised the Atlantic, north and south, and rounded Cape Horn at least once. He climbed up through the ranks of commercial seamanship and by 1802 was the master of the schooner *John B.* bound for the Turk Islands with a cargo of sheep. Familial constraints appear to have led him to a job on the Hudson River in the summer of 1814 where he heard about an army vacancy at Sackets. Desirous of seeing the war firsthand, he gained employment as commander of the U.S. Army Transport Service and travelled to Lake Ontario.

Pease's war experience was brief, but his journal offers insight into a little known aspect of the conflict, namely, the army's transport service.[22] He remained with that department for a short time after the war and then worked as master aboard lakers for one additional season. Pease kept journals throughout his life afloat and ashore. Some are daily logs, complete with pen and ink sketches of whales captured, while others are memoirs that include pilot's charts. It is obvious that Pease was as real a sea dog as any who came to the lake and regrettable that he did not join the action sooner, for the outcome might have been a memoir as informative as Ned Myers's narrative.

The accounts presented here are arranged in roughly chronological order. They begin with Richardson's description of conditions before the war and end with his and Pease's tales of what they did after the fighting had ended. In between, most of the significant events on Lake Ontario are described and analysed. Where Richardson fails to mention the "Burlington Races," Sinclair depicts the blow-by-blow action. When Kent curtly dispenses with the attack on Oswego, Richardson provides the details.

Hopefully, this collection of memoirs and letters will help the reader gain a better appreciation for how and why things developed as they did on Lake Ontario. Although no great, decisive naval action is portrayed here, insight into all the lesser incidents should help to make the puzzle of the war easier to understand. And who better to hear the stories from, than the men who lived to tell them?

Robert Malcomson
St. Catharines, Ontario

---

[22] The portion of Pease's journals used here is Journal 14, Spring 1814 to 19 August, 1815, Pease Papers, Department of Special Collections, Syracuse University Library. Additional, related information may be found in Journal 15. A summary of each volume of the series, prepared by library staff, was useful in compiling this brief biography.

Editor's Note

Although the differences among the source material of the following memoirs and letters required that the authors receive individual editorial treatment, it was possible to take some similar steps in dealing with them. New paragraphing was introduced to break up the density of the 19th century prose and to make the stories easier to comprehend. Major errors or inconsistencees in fact have been indicated in the notes. Spellings of the names of people, places and ships have been standardized according to current conventions.

The Sinclair and Pease narratives were taken from original sources, which featured many incorrect spellings of common vocabulary. These variant forms were left untouched unless the meaning of the content was threatened. As well, both men generally employed quickly scrawled dashes to break the text into sentence-like units, as was the contemporary practice. These have been removed and replaced with periods and new-sentence capital letters The original versions of the Richardson and Kent material probably featured similar variations

in spelling and sentence formation, but the editors who initially handled their narratives likely standardized the styles. Since the printed forms of their stories were used as sources for this volume, the spelling and most sentence breaks as originally published are used here, unimproved.

As noted in the Introduction, the Richardson "Reminiscences" was organized with little concern for chronology or flow. To make it more accessible, the article was re-arranged significantly to create a more even, less repetitious account of Richardson's experience. Ellipses have been used to signify breaks where text was reorganized or deleted.

The text notes, which are intended to clarify and complement the narratives, provide additional information on the persons, vessels, places and events mentioned in the main text. Where identification is not contained in a note, either insufficient direction was given in the main text to find the relevant information, or it was not available.

... R. M.

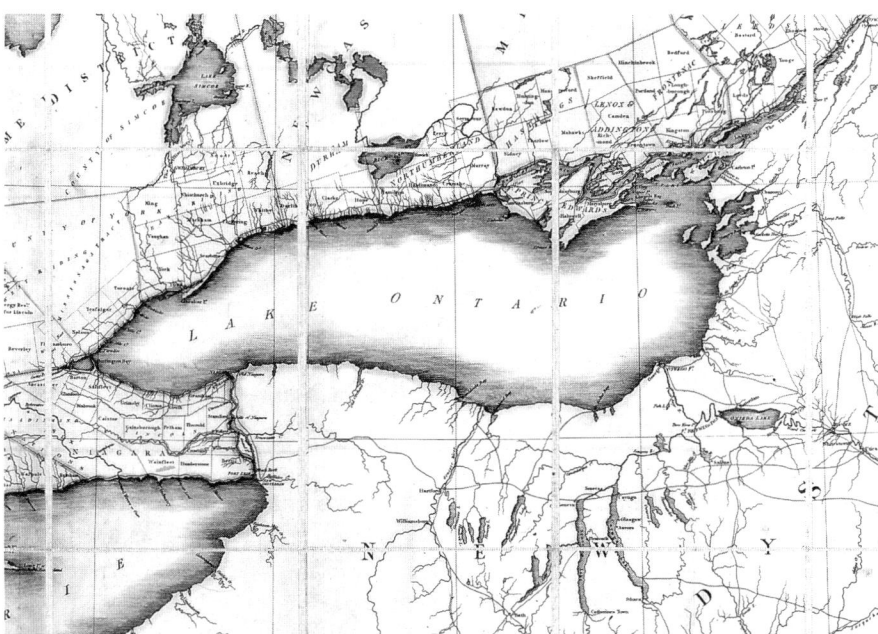

Lake Ontario and environs from a survey dated "January 1st 1813" by William Faden. *Courtesy, Archives of Ontario, Toronto.*

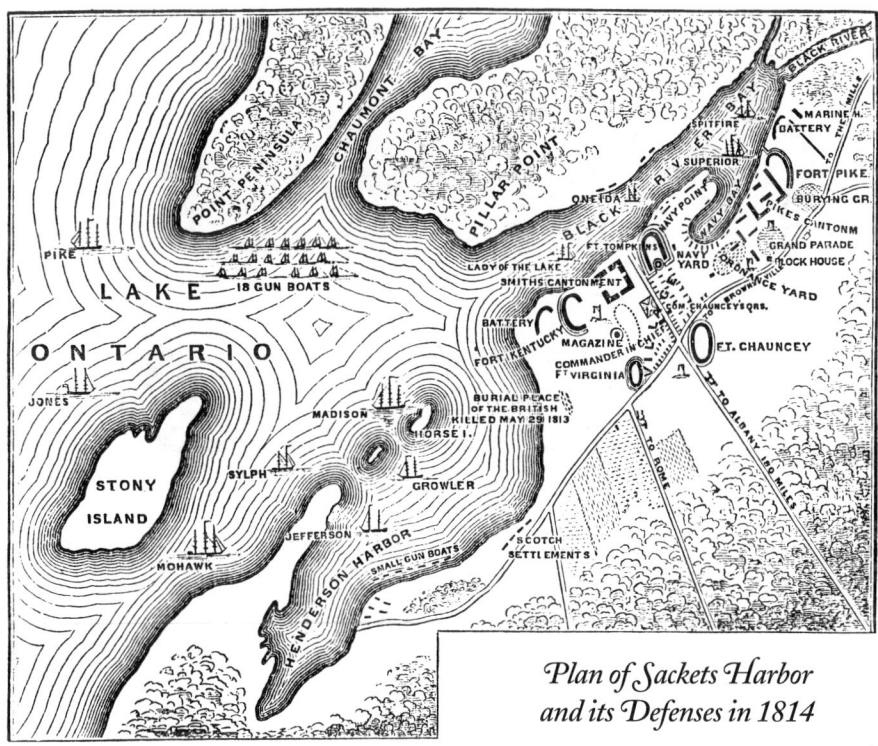

Plan of Sackets Harbor and its Defenses in 1814

Woodcut engraving from Benjamin J. Lossing's *Pictorial Field-book of the War of 1812.*

Master James RICHARDSON
Provincial Marine & Royal Navy

I.
The Memoirs of Master James Richardson,
Provincial Marine & Royal Navy
1812 - 1813

I was born in the town of Kingston, N. Y. on the 29th of January 1791. My father, James Richardson, was from Lincolnshire, near Horncastle, and my mother, Sarah Ashmore, was from Kings Norton, near Birmingham, in the County of Worcester.

In his early life, my father served in the Royal Navy and was in the *Ramillies*, 74, gunship, at the time she encountered the ever-memorable storm and disastrous gale [of] September 1782. After being dismasted and in a sinking state for five days, the vessel at last foundered, not, however, until all the officers and crew had been taken off by some merchant ships which had weathered the storm.

The ill-fated ship with several other men-of-war formed part of the West Indian Squadron under Lord Rodney. At the time mentioned they were convoying a homeward-bound fleet of merchantmen, with the prizes captured in the famous victory, over the fleet commanded by De Grasse.

Some of these prizes, such as the *Ville de Paris*, 120 guns; and the *Centaur*, 74 guns, were ships of the first class, but they, with several of the English men-of-war, went down together during the gale. The particulars of the fearful storm may be found recorded in the "Marine Chronicle", and other histories of Marine disasters.

About the year 1785 my father received an appointment[23] to the Lakes of Canada, as Lieutenant in the Provincial Marine organized for the two-fold purpose of fighting the enemy and transporting troops and stores, under the direction of the Quarter-Master-General, in the Forces in British America, the senior officer for the time being, in each lake, was styled Commodore. This marine establishment existed coeval, with the Conquest of Canada.

---

[23] The elder James Richardson (c. 1759-1832) left the service of the Provincial Marine around 1787 when he was hired by entrepreneur Richard Cartwright to build the schooner *Lady Dorchester*. He later commanded that laker and others, including the *Kingston Packet*, the *Elizabeth* and the *Governor Simcoe*. Richardson was at the helm of the latter schooner on 11 November 1812 when it reached Kingston after a narrow escape from Commodore Isaac Chauncey's squadron. He served in the squadron of Sir James Yeo until his discharge in October 1813. See *DCB*, vol. 6, pp. 638-9.

My earliest recollections are associated with it. Old Commodore Bouchette,[24] father of the late Surveryor-General of Lower Canada, I recollect as commanding at Kingston, when I was a boy.

1. Service with the Provincial Marine

At the age of 18, in 1809, I entered the Service, and in 1812 I received a commission as Lieutenant, being just turned 21 years.

The War with the United States commenced that year - our naval force on Lake Ontario consisted of the Ship *Royal George*,[25] 20 guns; the *Moira*,[26] 16 guns; the schooner *Duke of Gloucester*,[27] 18 guns; and, the schooner *Prince Regent*,[28] afterwards called the *Netley*, 12 guns; with a few smaller vessels doing service as gunboats and transports. Our Senior Officer was Commodore Hugh Earl.[29]

Our little squadron, though not very much celebrated for exploits in the way of fighting, managed, however, to keep open the communication between the

---

[24] Jean-Baptiste Bouchette (1736-1804) was given command of the Provincial Marine squadron on Lake Ontario on 1794, which he held until 1803.

[25] The *Royal George* was designed by John Dennis and launched at the Provincial Marine dockyard on Point Frederick at Kingston in July 1809. It was 101 feet long on its gundeck, 27 feet, 7 inches abeam and pierced for 20 guns. Various arrangements of carronades and long guns were carried on this vessel, and no attempt has been made here to explain each change, nor have ordnance arrangements been shown for most of the other vessels.

[26] The *Earl of Moira* was designed by John Dennis for the Provincial Marine and launched at Point Frederick in May 1805. It was 70 feet on the gundeck, 23 feet, 8 inches abeam and was pierced for 16 guns.

[27] The *Duke of Gloucester* was launched at Kingston in 1807. Its dimensions are unknown, although it appears to have been a small, schooner-rigged vessel. While undergoing extensive repairs at York in April 1813, it was captured by the Americans and towed to Sackets Harbor where it was re-named the *York*.

[28] The *Prince Regent* was designed by John Dennis for the Provincial Marine and launched at York in July 1812. It was 71 feet, 9 inches long on its gundeck, 21 feet abeam and was pierced for 12 guns. Schooner-rigged, the *Regent* was originally intended to replace the schooner *Toronto*, which had been used primarily by the government of the province of Upper Canada. Upon its launch, it was armed and attached to the Lake Ontario squadron. Its name was changed to the *Beresford* in May 1813 and to the *Netley* in May 1814, when a restructuring of the Royal Navy squadron resulted in name changes for most of the vessels.

[29] Hugh Earl (1765-1841) obtained a commission as a second lieutenant in the Provincial Marine in 1792. After the turn of the century he commanded the government yacht *Toronto* for several years. In 1812 he was advanced to master and commander and placed in charge of the Lake Ontario squadron aboard the *Royal George*.

Eastern and the Western Divisions of the Army, and to facilitate the transport of men and stores, as occasion required; as likewise the conveyance of the prisoners, which from time to time fell into the hands of our forces, during the first year of the war. The importance of such services in the then uninhabited state of the country, and the lack of land conveyance owing to the badness of the roads, must be obvious.

From some mistrust that the Provincial Marine would not be adequate to the increasing emergencies of the war, application was made[30] to the Admiralty of England for aid from the Royal Navy, and accordingly, in the Winter of 1812 Captain Barclay,[31] accompanied by Commanders Downie[32] and Pring,[33] Lieutenant Scott[34] and a few warrant officers and sailors were despatched from Halifax across the wilderness, through storms, posts and snowdrifts to Quebec; thence to Kingston, where they arrived in April; weather-beaten, exhausted and all but done-up.

Captain Barclay took the command until the arrival in May of Sir James Yeo,[35] direct from England with 500 officers and men.

---

[30] Although the Provincial Marine squadron provided transportation services, it failed to confront the threat posed by the small American squadron being developed on the lake. A haphazard attack was made on Sackets Harbor on 19 July 1812, but little else was attempted before Commodore Isaac Chauncey took control of the lake the following November.

[31] Robert Barclay (1785-1837) joined the Royal Navy in 1797. In March 1813 he was advanced to the rank of commander and selected at Bermuda by Admiral John Warren, to whom Sir George Prevost also appealed for help, to sail to Halifax and to travel overland from Saint John, New Brunswick to take charge at Kingston. Commodore Yeo superseded him there the following May, and sent Barclay to command the squadron on Lake Erie, which he lost to Master Commandant Oliver Hazard Perry's squadron on 10 September 1813 at Put-in-Bay.

[32] Captain George Downie (?-1814) did not accompany Barclay to Kingston. He was part of a 700-man detachment sent to the lakes from England in the spring of 1814. Commodore Yeo appointed him to command the squadron on Lake Champlain, which he lost to Master Commandant Thomas Macdonough's squadron on 11 September 1814 at Plattsburgh.

[33] Commander Daniel Pring (c. 1788-1846) was also promoted by Admiral Warren at Bermuda and sent with Barclay to the lakes. He was with Downie at Plattsburgh and acquitted in the court martial convened to examine the loss.

[34] Lieutenant John Scott was also promoted by Admiral Warren and sent with Barclay to the lakes. The rest of the men in Barclay's detachment were Commander Robert Finnis, Lieutenants John Garland, George Inglis, Robert Gibbes, Miller Worseley and Thomas Stokoe, and two gunners, Thomas Williams and Daniel Jack.

[35] Sir James Lucas Yeo (1782-1818) joined the Royal Navy in 1793. He was advanced to lieutenant in 1797, commander in 1805 and post captain in 1807. After he captured Cayenne from the French for the Portuguese, the prince regent of Portugal awarded him with a knighthood. He was also made a knight commander of the Bath by the British monarch. He was selected by the Admiralty to »»

"I had the honor of being despatched by Captain Barclay in the gun-boat Black Snake *to meet Sir James."*

I had the honour of being despatched by Captain Barclay in the gun-boat *Black Snake*[36] to meet Sir James,[37] with his flotilla of unarmed Canadian bateaux,[38] and escort him up the river, along the frontier of the enemy to Kingston. The scenes and feelings attendant on the discharge of the duty — having a small flat-bottomed craft with about 8 men and a three-pounder in the bow, to pass for sixty miles on open frontier of the enemy, mostly in the night, called for a sharp look-out, with both nerve and caution. No enemy, however, appeared, and we returned unmolested with the rear division under Captain Mulcaster[39] in the latter part of May 1813.

The naval armaments on the lakes now assumed a new character and position, no longer Provincial, but part of the Royal Navy.

Our Provincial Commissions were of no force in the new relations, yet because of our local knowledge and experience, our services were desirable, and required by our new Commodore. None, however of the Commissioned Officers on Lake Ontario consented to remain, except Lieutenant George Smith[40] and myself. I told the Commodore that if my services were of any avail, they were at his command, only I would not take any rank inferior to that I held in the Provincial Marine. He remarked that the rules of the Service precluded my relation as a lieutenant among them, but would rate me accordingly. This, while it gave me rank in the "gun-room"[41] with the commissioned officers, would be appropriate to the two-fold duties of Master and Pilot.

»» lead the Royal Navy detachment, numbering 466 officers and men, sent to Canada in response to Sir George Prevost's appeal for naval assistance. The detachment left England on 30 March 1813 and arrived at Quebec on 5 May. Yeo reached Kingston on 15 May.

[36] The *Black Snake* was one of as many as two dozen different gunboats that operated out of Kingston during the war. It was 44 feet in length, 8 feet, 6 inches abeam, with fittings for 22 sweeps, or oars, and a single gun mounted in its bows. The *Black Snake* was captured and scuttled in the St. Lawrence River south of Wolfe Island by the Americans in June 1814, but was later salvaged by the British.

[37] Richardson apparently met Yeo's detachment at Prescott, a village located about sixty miles down the St. Lawrence River. The Royal Navy detachment travelled to Kingston by boat and afoot in three separate divisions.

[38] Bateaux varied in size and were powered chiefly by oars and simple rigs. They were managed by the Commissariat Department of the army. Local inhabitants were contracted to crew the bateaux, although militia units or the passengers themselves were frequently the only rowers available.

[39] Commander William Mulcaster (1785-1837) joined the Royal Navy in 1793 as an eight year old volunteer and was promoted to lieutenant by the age of fifteen. In 1809 he was the first lieutenant aboard Yeo's *Confiance* and played an important role in the capture of the French base at Cayenne for which he was advanced to the rank of commander.

[40] George Smith was recommended by Hugh Earl as "an old steady seaman." See Report by Andrew Gray, 24 February 1812, NAC, RG 8, I, "C series", vol. 728, p. 86.

In this highly responsible relation I continued to serve, to the best of my ability, during the remainder of the war, and for some time after, sharing the fatigues, dangers and exploits of the campaigns of 1813 and 1814 of which the published narratives of the war furnish details.

The building of ships at the Kingston dockyards calls for a passing remark: During the season of 1812, while the Provincial Marine existed, the *Wolfe*,[42] a corvette of twenty guns, was built and commissioned, also the *Melville*[43] of sixteen guns. These added materially to the strength of our naval armament at the time Sir James Yeo took command. The Americans also kept adding to their strength. The fine commodious ship *Pike*,[44] 28 guns, with the *Madison*[45] of 32, were launched in the Spring of 1813....

2. John Dennis, the Ship Builder

While speaking of ship-building I must not forget to mention that in the summer of 1812 Mr. John Dennis, then the master-builder in the dockyard at Kingston was ordered to York (now Toronto) to build a ship with which he had proceeded during the winter, so that she was nearly completed in April 1813, when the place fell into the hands of the enemy, who burnt her on the stocks.[46] The officers and attachees of the dockyard formed into a Company

---

[41] The gunroom was the officers' wardroom or "mess" aboard small vessels. It was a space in the rear of the ship below the quarterdeck, ahead of the captain's cabin, and lined on either side with tiny cabins for the commissioned officers, senior warrant officers and midshipmen.

[42] The *Wolfe*, was designed by Thomas Plucknett and launched at Point Frederick on 28 April 1813. It was originally named the *Sir George Prevost*, which name was changed almost immediately. The corvette was built to resemble the *Royal George*, although it was 107 feet long on the gundeck, 30 feet, 10 inches abeam and pierced for 22 guns.

[43] The *Lord Melville* was designed by George Record and launched at Point Frederick in July 1813. It was a brig that measured 72 feet, 10 inches on the gundeck, 24 feet, 3 inches abeam and was pierced for 14 guns.

[44] The *General Pike* was designed by Henry Eckford (1775-1832) and launched at Sackets Harbor on 12 June 1813. It was a corvette that measured about 145 feet on the gundeck with a breadth of about 39 feet and it was pierced for 26 guns.

[45] The *Madison* was designed by Henry Eckford and launched at Sackets Harbor on 26 November 1812, the first vessel built by that industrious master shipwright at Sackets. It was a corvette that measured about 112 feet on the gundeck, 32 feet abeam and was pierced for 22 guns.

[46] On 26 April 1813, the American squadron landed 1800 infantrymen at York who succeeded in capturing the town. After a stiff defense, the British commander, Major General Sir Roger Hale Sheaffe, ordered his surviving infantry to retreat from the town after setting fire to the frigate *Sir Isaac Brock*, which stood partially built in the dockyard.

of which Mr. Dennis, the master-builder[47] was Captain. This Company aided to the utmost of their power in defending the place, but being with the other forces, overpowered, they had to share in the discomfiture....

At the close of the war which gave the States their independence, Mr. Dennis, who in the meantime had married in New York, Martha Brown, the widow of Surgeon McClany, of the Royal Navy, who had perished at sea in the frigate to which he belonged, was sent with other of the Loyalists to "Beaver Harbour," Nova Scotia. This proving a barren, inhospitable place he could barely sustain his family and therefore seeking more favorable parts he at length migrated to Upper Canada about the time that Governor Simcoe had surveyed and began to settle the fertile land in the vicinity of Toronto. He drew his portion on the banks of the Humber, a few miles from the site of the present village of Weston. Here for some years he had to grub and toil and suffer the privations incident to the formation of settlements in the wilderness without even a road from the "town" or rather the then "town-plot" to his dwelling, having to "pad" it along the lake shore and banks of the Humber, carrying, perchance, a few pounds of flour or other necessaries, on his back, to keep life in the family.

Being a ship-builder, he occasionally, during his residence in this isolated spot, built small vessels for such as required them, among others a neat Government yacht called the *Toronto*,[48] a schooner rigged for the transit of officers and employees of the Government, with others, across the Lake, which proved a great convenience and pleased his Excellency Governor Hunter[49] so well that he gave him the appointment of Master-Builder in the King's Dockyard at Kingston about the year 1802; where he continued till at the outbreaking of the war he was removed to York to build the ship before-mentioned.

Here he continued to reside until August 1832, when he fell victim to cholera, in the 73rd year of his age. His son, Joseph Dennis, Esquire, and grandson of Henry Dennis, now holds and resides on the property he left on

---

[47] John Dennis (1758-1832) was not the master-builder of the frigate *Sir Isaac Brock* at York during the winter and spring of 1813. As part of the re-location of the Provincial Marine headquarters to York from Kingston, a "shake up" in the administration of the Marine Department was enacted. A master builder from Quebec named Thomas Plucknett was recommended to Sir George Prevost who chose him to design the *Brock* and the *Wolfe*. Plucknett was in charge of the project at York and Dennis was his foreman. Plucknett proved to be so incompetent that army officers overseeing the project were bypassing him and giving their instructions to Dennis at the time of the American attack.

[48] The *Toronto* was launched in 1799 at York.

[49] Peter Hunter (1746-1805) was appointed in 1799 to be commander in chief of the forces in Canada and the lieutenant governor of Upper Canada, positions he held until his death.

the banks of the Humber, not now, however, in the heart of a wilderness, isoloated and forlorn; but a beautiful county-seat contiguous....

It was while Mr. Dennis resided as Master-Builder at the said dockyard that I became acquainted with his daughter Rebecca and subsequently made her the steadfast partner of my life....

3. The Attack on Sackets Harbor, 29 May 1813

The failure of the expedition against Sackets Harbor,[50] under the immediate command of the General-in-Chief, Sir George Prevost[51], which opened the Campaign of 1813, is wholly inexplicable.

Why were not the troops landed in the forenoon of the day of our appearance off this place, when the wind and weather, and every other circumstance were favorable, when none of the enemy were at the landing place (respecting which I had the honour of being consulted) to oppose, when our men were in the boats and the anchors were ready to be dropped?

Instead of landing and taking the place, which probably could have been effected without the loss of five men, the men were ordered to embark and the ships were hauled to the wind,[52] and were made to stand off till midnight; then, in the dark, at the distance of several miles, the men were put into the boats and ordered to find their way, as best they could, to the same landing-place, abreast which they had been in the morning. In the meantime the enemy had posted themselves, had fortified their position, had received large reinforcements by land and water during the day, and were prepared to give us a warm reception.

---

[50] A British force including about 800 infantrymen sailed from Kingston after dark on 27 May in five warships and more than 30 bateaux and gunboats bound for an attack on Sackets Harbor. They arrived off the port the next day, but adverse winds and vacillating orders inhibited the attack until dawn on 29 May. Colonel Edward Baynes, Adjutant General of the armed forces in B. N. A., was in charge of the mission, although Sir George Prevost, who was present in the squadron and on the battlefield, appears to have been very influential in the decisions made. The British were opposed by about 1400 regular and militia American troops, led by Lieutenant Colonel Electus Backus and Brigadier General Jacob Brown. See Patrick Wilder, *The Battle of Sackett's Harbour, 1813*, (Baltimore, 1994).

[51] Sir George Prevost (1767-1816) entered the army in 1779 and rose to command British forces at St. Vincent in 1794. He later served as lieutenant governor of St. Vincent, St. Lucia, Dominica and Nova Scotia. He became governor-in-chief and captain general of the British forces in B. N. A. in 1811. His headquarters was at Quebec, although he frequently moved nearer to the front during the war.

[52] The spars were pulled around so that the sails were set nearer to the direction of the wind. In this case the squadron turned away from the shore and slowly headed back to open water.

Why was it that after several hours of hard fighting, and great sacrifice of life, when the enemy had been driven from their works, and were in the act of abandoning the place, and had in despair, actually set fire to their own navy-yard and store-houses, was a retreat sounded, the troops re-embarked, and the dead, with some of the wounded left to the enemy, is a question left to this day a mystery. I heard one of our brave colonials, as he came up the ship's side, indignantly exclaim; "Oh, if he would but give me my own regiment, I would yet land again and take the place."[53]

A somewhat amusing incident occurred in the afternoon of the day; while our ship was working to windward away from the landing-place as above mentioned, and yet about six miles distant in the offing, a boat was observed coming towards us from a point of land covered with bush, which forms the entrance of a deep bay called Henderson's Harbor, distant from us about one and a half miles, displaying a flag of truce. Lieut. Dobbs[54] was sent with one of the ship's boats to meet the American and know his business. The boats met and after a short time we observed one boat with Lieut. Dobbs proceed to the shore, while the American stood toward us.

Commodore Yeo suspected a Yankee trick of some sort; but not so, it turned out to be an honest, but not very brave affair, for he was soon alongside and being interrogated by Lieut. Owen,[55] the officer on duty, as to his business. He said he was a captain of Dragoons, and had come off with his men to surrender and claim our protection as prisoners of war against the savages on the shore, that the woods were full of Indians, that he had had a fight with them that morning; and rather than fall into their hands and be massacred, he surrendered to us, that there was another boat-load of his men that would come under the escort of our officer. The lieutenant on duty reported the message to the Commodore, who was with Sir George Prevost and Staff at dinner, and orders were given to receive them on board. Lieutenant Owen therefore replied, "Very

---

[53] Prevost was the "he" of this quote. The muttering about Prevost's influence on the timing of the attack and the retreat spread throughout the army and navy corps as one participant, Lieutenant John Le Couteur, 104th Regiment, recollected: "It was a scandalously managed affair. We gained a surprise and threw it away to allow the enemy to gain time. The murmurs against Sir George were deep, not loud." See Donald Graves (ed.), *Merry Hearts Make Light Days: The War of 1812 Journal of Lieutenant John Le Couteur, 104th Foot* (Ottawa, 1993), p. 117. See also Frederick Drake, "Commodore Sir James Lucas Yeo and Governor General George Prevost: A Study in Command Relations, 1813-14", *New Interpretations in Naval History: Selected Papers from the Eighth Naval History Symposium*, William B. Cogar (ed.), (Annapolis, 1989), pp. 156-171.

[54] Alexander Dobbs (1784-1827) entered the Royal Navy in 1797. He was promoted to lieutenant in 1804 and commander in 1814.

[55] Charles Cunliffe Owen entered the Royal Navy in 1801. He was promoted to lieutenant in 1807 and commander in 1814 and became a close friend of Commodore Yeo.

"... my heart is as square as any man's."

well, Sir", and the brave captain with his men were safely secured, and assured of our protection, his fears no doubt subsided. He was a portly-built man armed to the teeth, with a hanger by his side and a pair of pistols on his belt, etc. He was then ushered into the presence of the Commodore and officers at the dinner table. Whether the countenances of any present gave indication of surprise or suspicion at this most extraordinary surrender I cannot say, but he must have observed some tokens of this kind, for it was reported by the officer who introduced him to the cabin, that he uttered this queer remark: "Gentlemen I confess my appearance is rather uncouth, but my heart is as square as any man's."

In a short time the other boat with his men were alongside and safely accommodated with quarters on board — the whole mustered about thirty unmounted Dragoons. They were on their way to Sackets with the boats and having encamped on the point in the night, had an encounter with two or three canoe loads of Chippewa Indians, perhaps a dozen or so, who had accompanied the expedition from Kingston.[56] The Indians had got the worst of it and had retreated from the place altogether — one of them was wounded and was then in the ship with his thigh shot, so that for several hours the dastardly Dragoons had not an enemy near when he sought our protection, nor had we even noticed, much less molested him during the day — so much for the power of imagination acting as nervous timidity. The dread of encounter with Indian foes was a striking feature among many of the Americans and it evinced itself in several instances during the late war. To the effect of nursery tales and fireside legends aided by "thrilling narratives" issuing from a mercenary press the Americans are most indebted for this weakness.

Some of us were ungenerous enough to think that this instance of pussilanimity on the part of the enemy had its influence on the Commodore to induce him to return to the attack on Sackets, as before mentioned. But of this conjecture I cannot speak, I give merely the facts as they occurred....

4. Raiding the American Shore

Our Commodore, in the absence of something to fight,[57] proceeded to inspect the enemies' coasts and harbors in search of provisions, and being informed that the United States had a large stock of flour, deposited in the village of Big Sodus about 30 miles west of Oswego, he brought his squadron

---

[56] Lieutenant ColonelThomas Aspinwall, 9th U. S. Infantry Regiment, was in charge of 250 infantrymen from the 9th and 21st U.S. Infantry Regiments who were hurrying by bateaux to reinforce the post at Sackets. They were intercepted by about three dozen Mississauga and Mohawk warriors operating from the British squadron in canoes. In all, 115 Americans from Aspinwall's detachment surrendered in this incident.

"... a flash of lightning ... showed whom we were."

to anchor, and toward evening[58] sent in the boats with a few sailors and detachment of about 60 of the Royals.[59] It became dark before we made the landing, and an advance party of fifteen, of which I was one, commanded by Captain Mulcaster, proceeded at once to the village, under guidance of one acquainted with the place.

We found the houses deserted, and not a person to be seen, but one in a tavern so drunk that we could get no information from him. After seeking in vain for the inhabitants, during which strict orders were given not to molest any furniture or private property, and while our Captain was consulting as to future proceedings, it being very dark, someone hailed us from some bushes close by. Captain Mulcaster answered "Friend", but before the word was fully out, they fired a volley, which felled five of our fifteen. They then took themselves off. The detachment of the Royals coming up in our rear, having heard the firing, took us for the enemy, and also discharged a few shots at us before the mistake was discovered.

Captain Wilson[60] of the Royals who was among the fifteen in advance, wore a peculiarly- shaped cocked hat, which a flash of lightning, happily for our party, revealed and showed whom we were.

The enemy was no more seen during the night, but towards morning some stragglers came within the line of our sentry and were arrested. Being questioned as to the firing, as also, where the inhabitants of the village were, they said that the inhabitants themselves fired; that on the approach of the ships in the evening, a consultation was held in the village and while some would have remained quietly at home, under the conviction that they would not be molested, the majority decided to arm themselves and fire on us, some of them remarking that they would have the satisfaction of killing some British anyway.[61]

---

[57] Commodore Chauncey had been busily occupied from late April to late May with transporting and supplying the army during its campaign at the western end of the lake. After the attack on Sackets, Chauncey kept his squadron there through most of June and July as he waited for the preparation of his new ship, the *General Pike*. During this period Yeo's squadron cruised the lake, more or less unmolested.

[58] The British arrived at Sodus around 7:00 P. M. on 19 June 1813.

[59] A detachment of the Royal Scots, or the 1st Regiment of Foot, was serving in the British squadron as marines.

[60] Captain John Wilson of the 1st Battalion of Royal Scots.

[61] A militia officer named William Bennett led a company of about 40 militiamen to oppose the British landing. The fighting took place during a heavy shower of rain.

This word having come to the Commodore he ordered the place to be burnt, as a warning to all others along the coast.[62]

The prisoners being liberated, were instructed to say that wherever we came, if the inhabitants remained quiet, private property and rights would be respected, but, in all cases, where the people made armed resistance and wantonly fired on us, they might expect to be punished in like manner.

All we got in return for our visit was about 500 barrels of flour, found in a storehouse.

I have since conversed with an American gentleman, who was at this place at the time, who said that about 8,000 barrels[63] of flour belonging to the United States were concealed in the woods, which were not discovered because of the blackness of the night.

5. The Failed Cutting-Out Expedition

...In the month of July 1813, the Americans having launched and fitted out the *Pike* and the *Madison*, previously mentioned, had them at anchor outside the point forming the entrance to Sackets Harbor. Commodore Yeo conceived the design of a "cut out," by stealing a march on them in the night[64], with a number of armed men in boats manned by expert seamen, with a detachment of the 100th Regiment and a few marines, under the command of Major Hamilton.[65]

---

[62] The burning of Sodus also alarmed British citizens, as one correspondent at York stated to Sir George Prevost: "there is some regret expressed that it became necessary for the Commodore to destroy the town of Sodus from the apprehension that this place may be the subject of retaliation." (See Powell to Prevost, 28 June 1813, NAC, RG 8, I, "C Series", vol. 679, p.148.) When Commodore Chauncey's squadron visited York between 31 July and 2 August the commodore remarked to a representative of the town that "his coming to York at present was a sort of retribution for the visits our fleet made on the other side of the lake and to possess himself of the public stores and destroy the fortifications, but he would burn no house." (See Powell and Strachan to Freer, 2 August 1813, NAC, RG 8, I, "C Series," vol. 679:324.) On 2 August the Americans burned the barracks, woodyard and storehouses on Gibraltar Point, across the bay from York. This trail of burnings would lead eventually to President Madison's mansion in Washington.

[63] A published report of the time indicated that 800 barrels had been hidden by Bennett and his men. The British reported that 230 barrels of flour were seized.

[64] Around 5:00 P. M. on 30 June 1813 Commodore Yeo led a flotilla of boats containing most of the seamen in his squadron, plus detachments of the 100th Regiment and the Royal Scots, from the squadron anchored in Kingston south toward Sackets Harbor. His intention was to attack the American base at dawn and "cut out" some of his vessels, that is, capture them and sail them back to Kingston.

[65] Major Christopher Hamilton of the 100th Regiment of Foot.

Accordingly we left Kingston about 5 o'clock p.m., expecting to reach the ships before daylight next morning, the distance being about 40 miles.

Such, however, was the sluggishness of some of the gunboats, propelled by oars, that notwithstanding the calmness of the night, the daylight began to dawn as we rounded the point which opened out the ships at anchor, about eight miles distant. It would not answer to approach them in daylight, and to attempt retreat would have been equally fatal, for, had we been discovered they might have overhauled us and blown us to atoms. No expedient was therefore left us but to hide in some nook or corner of the shore, which was covered with a dense wood, and be concealed, if possible, till the next night.

Our Commodore, therefore, proceeded ahead to scent, and found such a place about two miles up the mouth of Hungry Bay, to which we retired, and having laid the boats broadside to the beach of a shall bend in the shore, we cut saplings and bushes, and placed them in the water outside the boats, by means of which we were tolerably well screened. Our force numbered about 700 officers and men, and strict orders were given not to kindle any fires, or raise a smoke, or discharge any firearm, but to keep quietly concealed in the woods till darkness should favour us. During the day boats passed, and the enemy's armed schooners continued sailing to and fro between us and the open lake, but failed to discern us, which had they done, we should doubtless have had our boats destroyed, and we left fugitives in an enemy's land, which was covered with forest trees for several miles on either side. We were destitute of firearms, except a few, as we were not permitted to depend but on our swords, cutlasses, boarding-axes and pikes for the execution of the work. In such a dilemma as that our ingenuity would have been fully tested, but fortunately it was not put to the test.

We escaped the notice of the enemy, but, alas! not the treachery of some of our own party. Some time after we had made good our landing, when the muster roll was called, a sergeant and a private of the 100th were discovered to be missing; search was made in the woods without avail, and it became evident they had taken themselves off, but as there was no house between ten and twelve miles, and they were strangers in the country, hopes were entertained that they would not be able to betray us before nightfall.

Our Commodore was evidently much exercised in mind through the day, lest his enterprise should be baffled, and conversed with me as having more local knowledge of these parts, relative to the practicability of their finding their way to some inhabitants and thus giving the alarm.

Just before sundown, one of the armed schooners, which had been standing off and on, about a mile to the westward between us and the point, anchored and sent her boat to shore, and when it returned, she fired an alarm gun and made sail directly to Sackets Harbor.

We had no doubt that the villainous deserters had shown themselves on the beach, which proved to be the case.[66] The chagrin and disappointment caused by this betrayal, and the consequent failure of our scheme, within a few hours of what would probably have been its successful termination, may be conceived. We all felt it sorely, but Commodore Yeo could hardly restrain himself. Nothing could be done but seek our own safe retreat.

As soon as night set in we were ordered to embark, and, putting into the offing, got sight of the ships, which were fully lighted up, and prepared to give us a warm reception, if we had the audacity to make the attack. Orders were given to pull for the Canadian side, and by day-break next morning we saw the American squadron under full sail after us, but the wind was so light during the night that they did not come up, and we reached Kingston in safety.

After the war was over I was informed, in conversation with an American officer, that, the day we lay concealed, a pleasure party of ladies and gentlemen had been regaling themselves on Stony Island in the lake some miles beyond where we were, and when they returned home in the evening and were told that a force of 700 Britishers were the whole day between them and their homes, some the ladies nearly fainted....

In regard to Sir James Yeo and Commodore Chauncey, who though frequently in the vicinity of each other, and exchanging shots in partial combats, never came to any decisive action, free opinions and doubts of fidelity and courage have been thrown out. I may by way of explanation, explain: Sir James Yeo had mostly short carronades, which though adapted to rapid firing, were not suited to long range, while, on the other hand, Chauncey had long guns which gave him a decided advantage at a distance. In consequence the one was anxious to seek close quarters while it was the policy of the other to keep his distance. As the closing in action with sailing vessels depends on the "weather gauge",[67] a decisive action was avoided on each side as the circumstances alternated.

It is but due to the memory of Sir James Yeo to state that I heard him say, on a certain occasion of avoiding the enemy, in reply to a suggestion of Captain Mulcaster, that if he had his command on the high seas, he would risk an action at all hazards, because, should he be beaten, it would be but the loss of his

---

[66] Apart from the soldiers from the 100th Regiment, two seamen, James Hanlan and Baptiste Georgie, deserted while the British hid in the woods near Hungry Bay.

[67] During the preliminary stages of a naval battle, each opposing commander attempted to sail a course that would allow him to take a position upwind of his opponent. From this position, referred to as the "weather" or "wind gauge", a commander could sail down, with the wind at his stern to meet his enemy. Having lost the weather gauge, the opponent could flee, attempt an approach by sailing against the wind or wait for his enemy to sail down wind to him.

squadron, but to lose it in this lake, would involve the embarrassment, if not the discomfiture of the Western division of the army, whose dependence was on keeping open the channel of communication — so high a responsibility resting upon him he had to act with the more caution and prudence.[68]

"... the enemy's armed schooners continued sailing to and fro."

---

[68] The fact that the majority of ordnance in the British squadron was composed of short-ranged carronades while the Americans had a preponderance of long guns affected the tactics used by both commodores. Another observer of this point was David Wingfield, a British master's mate who had come to Canada with Yeo: "his [Yeo's] object was to engage them at close quarters and board, which would, in all human probability, have insured success: the Americans, on the contrary, were armed with long guns, and wanted to engage at a distance, out of range of our carronades, being fully informed of the state of our ships, as well as of our object: both sides were eager to engage, but neither would commence, without the advantage of the weather gage." See NAC, MG 24, F 18.

Captain Arthur SINCLAIR
United States Navy

II.
Private Correspondence of Captain Arthur Sinclair
United States Navy
1813

United States Ship *Gen'l Pike* Sackets Harbor
July the 4th 1813

Dear Jack:[69]

I received your welcome letter by our last Mail and am pleased once again to have it in my power to renew a correspondence with a friend I have always so highly valued, but who's silence and reserve for the few last years, has prevented that free and friendly intercourse which was formed in our early days, grew with us, and has always been the first wish of my heart to continue undiminished.

You mention the loss of the *Chesapeake*.[70] We have at last heard something of the particulars. It is stated that Capt Lawrence[71] received two wounds in the first broad side and was mortally wounded the second. The quarter deck was nearly cleared - yet the *Chesapeake* had evidently the advantage until in attempting to thwart the Enemy's bows to rake her the judgement of the Capt was wanting, as he had commenced the manoeuvre, and she fell onboard her. The *Shannon* had nearly the whole of the crew of the *Tenedos*,[72] in addition to her own and overpowered by boarding her.

---

[69] John Hartwell Cocke (1780-1866) was the brother of Arthur Sinclair's first wife, Elizabeth, who died in 1803 along with their twin children.

[70] The USS *Chesapeake*, 36, was captured in a ship-to-ship action against HMS *Shannon*, 38, captained by Philip B. V. Broke, on 1 June 1813 off Boston. The actual strength of the two ships was: *Chesapeake*, 50; *Shannon*, 52.

[71] James Lawrence (1781-1813) had served in the US Navy since 1798. After suffering his wounds during the battle with the *Shannon*, Lawrence is reputed to have said, "Don't give up the ship" as he was carried below to the surgeon. His friend, Oliver Hazard Perry, had these words stitched into a flag which he flew when he led his squadron into battle against the British on Lake Erie in September 1813.

[72] HMS *Tenedos*, 38, Captain Hyde Parker, had been patrolling the American coast in company »»

The cruizing ship has decidely the advantage of the one immediately out of port let her discipline be whatever it may. I do not offer any of those causes as apologies. The facts speak for themselves. The *Shannon* and *Acasta*[73] are two [of] the finest Frigates in the British service and have had their metal changed and an additional number added to their crews, making them exactly equal to Our largest class ships, which are as superior to the *Chesapeake's* class, as she is to a large class sloop of war. Alas! my poor friend Lawrence, nothing but death could deprive him of his Laurels. Our service has lost an excellent officer. He possest a sincere, friendly and excellent heart, will be much mist by Society, and his wife and children will feel his loss most sensibly.

I think you have misconstrued the motive of the Enemy in their attack on this place,[74] by believing it was to draw our troops from above. Their object was to destroy the new ship then on the stocks, which was all important to them, in as much, as she gives the balance of power in the Lakes.

When I look back and reflect on the generalship of our armies, I really cannot have any patience with those who have the direction, but it appears to me that everything like energy, enterprise and judgment had forsaken them, or that they never possest either. We had better make peace than carry on the war as we have done. It is in the first place but one continued routine of expense recruiting men for twelve months, for before they are disciplined and made to look like soldiers they are discharged, and thus the bounty and pay, which is so liberal, has been thrown away upon a worthless class of citizens without the least benefit to the nation.

Last winter when we had three thousand men at this place and the enemy not more than 3 or 400, and those provincial troops. Their navy maned in the same way and froze up at Kingston, what an opportunity did this offer to make us masters of the River St. Lawrence, which is all important both to us and them? The Ice was four feet thick on the Lake, our troops, artillery and horse paraded on it every day. Colnl Macomb[75] was anxious to have gone over - he commanded here; Genl Dearborn[76] forbid it. By getting their navy, at that time it would have saved the monstrous expense of building the two large ships

---

»» with the *Shannon* since April 1813. On 25 May Philip Broke ordered Parker to leave the area and to patrol independently until 14 June when they would rendezvous. Broke's reason was to encourage James Lawrence to sail out of Boston to do battle. Only casks of fresh water and provisions were transferred from the *Tenedos* to the *Shannon* before they parted company.

[73] HMS *Acasta*, 40, Captain J. P. Beresford.

[74] The British attack at Sackets Harbor on 29 May 1813.

[75] Colonel Alexander Macomb (1782-1841) was the military commander at Sackets Harbor during part of the winter 1813.

we now have. Kingston would have given complete command of everything passing up the St. Lawrence - besides the destruction or possession of their grand arsanal and depo for the upper province.

Now you see the effects of it. They have built a large 32 gun ship there, and have now another of 20 guns, and a number of large gunboats almost ready for service. They have brought up as many prime seamen as they want - 1500 marines and have now at Kingston 5,000[77] regular troops. The taking of Kingston, and the Navy which was perfectly in our power at that time would have now made us masters of this upper province. It is only 30 miles from this, a number of Islands for stopping places, and the Ice afforded a landing whenever we pleased. Now they are whining for it and cant get it. The lake is theirs until my ship[78] is ready, and I feel confident that they consider it of too much importance to risque a battle with us which we shall offer them in about three weeks, until they get their other vessels added to their present force, which will again give them the ascendancy. So it now seems to be the warfare of who can build faster, or run the other to the greatest expense.

A most daring enterprise was attempted the night before last[79] by Sir James Yeo - commander of their naval forces there. He left Kingston in the evening with 30 or 40 large boats with from 20 to 30 men each; but finding night would leave him before he could get here, he put on shore behind the point of a long peninsula, making out from between two Bays, about 8 miles from this Harbour. He there hauled up his boats, covered them with boughs of trees and secreted his men in the woods. One of his men fortunately deserted, and in crossing the bay on a plank was taken up by a canoe and brought up to us, otherwise he had two days walk through the wilderness to have gotten here, and in the meantime the object might have been effected; for although we keep guard Boats rowing every night and a vessel cruizing across the Bay, which has made us feel secure in the Fleet, yet that enterprising fellow, we are told, has

---

[76] Major General Henry Dearborn (1751-1829) was in charge of the American forces in Niagara at the time of Sinclair's letter, although on 6 July Secretary of War John Armstrong asked for Dearborn's resignation.

[77] Sinclair apparently refers to the *Wolfe*, 22, the *Melville*, 14 and to the 466 Royal Navy officers and men who had arrived with Commodore Yeo at Kingston. By this date, Sinclair and the rest of the American squadron had yet to see the 1813 version of the British squadron. "Intelligence" gained from informants and spies was often misleading.

[78] Sinclair had been sent to Sackets specifically for the purpose of taking command of the *General Pike*.

[79] This was the cutting-out expedition that was launched by the British on 30 June and aborted late on 1 July 1813, described by Richardson in Part I.

"One of his men fortunately deserted..."

been two nights in among us reconnoitering in his gigg, and past by answering *guard Boat*, when challenged by the shipping.

The man got to camp about 5 o'clock in the evening. The Comdr and myself were dining at head quarters and the plan was immediately fixed for their reception; but mine was to have acted on the offensive, and they now agree with me. I proposed embarking 1000 men headed by Colnl Macomb to be landed in the Bay nearest us, and high up towards the peninsula, for us then to go without the Point and opposite to them on the other side the Bay with the Squadron. There being a wilderness between the two they would not have known the troops were in their rear, and would no doubt have destroyed their Boats, and attempted to retreat by land, in either event, land or water they must have been ours, and then as their fleet were unmanned we might have returned them the complement intended us the next day, as our Boats might easily have been made to pass for theirs and our ships might have also gone in as prizes and taken their whole fleet with much ease. I was over ruled and we were moored, and after dark, in a proper line of defence, and our decks, secretly, manned with troops, principally riflemen, and every sailor a musket to resort to after the first broad side from our great guns. We should no doubt have (thus prepared) destroyed nearly all of them; but, as I expected, their secret agents here got wind of it and as soon as dark came an Indian canoe was dispatched to inform they were betrayed as we since have learned by others who deserted, and some who got lost, and came in as prisoners of war. Thus foiled they abandoned the Enterprise and returned to Kingston.

We went out with the Fleet at day light but were too late. The Comdr was fearful my ship would be carried by them in his absence in case he had have gone out the evening before; but light as she is, and so very high out of water without rigging or anything to assist them, it would have been impossible to have gained her deck under the fire of 4 or 500 soldiers, as I then had onboard. I would have defied their whole army in Boats to have made good a landing on my decks. What a glorious chance to have cut him off and become at once masters of the Lakes and all their naval force at one blow. I fear such another will never offer. Oh! for a little more management. Our Comdr does not want either for enterprise or courage, and when we meet them we shall give a good account of them, we shall be out as soon as my Ship is ready and if they meet us the fight will be a hard one no doubt.

I want to take this gallant Knight. I will if I do so, *bring him to Virginia in a Cage and shew him as a curiosity. How would he pass in your quarters?* But joking apart I expect d____d hard knocks. They have more guns in their fleet than we

---

[80] As of 4 July, the date of this letter, Sinclair had not seen the British fleet. His information about its strength is based on hearsay and is quite inßaccurate. Commodore Yeo eventually met the Americans with two ships, two brigs and two schooners, carrying 97 guns in all.

have but we as yet, with the new Ship, out number them.[80] They have the *Genl Wolfe* of 32 guns, - some 68 pdr Carronades, the *Royal George* of 24 - 32 pdr - 2 - 18 gun Brigs and 6 or 8 schooners. We have the *Genl Pike* of 28 guns long 24 pounders (the same the *Constellation*[81] had when we took the *Insurgente*), the *Madison* of 24 - 32 pdr Carronades, *Oneida* of 18 guns and 10 schooners with long 32 pdr, 18 pdr & 24 pdr.

When I hear from you again, I will answer your letter with a description of this new country upon this wonderful fresh water ocean. The land is delightful and covered with a monstrous growth of Timber - principally Elm - Cedar - White Oak of a very superior quality - Ash, Hemlock and white pine. The soil is black and light apparently formed of vegetable matter, and about the lakes it is about 3 feet deep to a solid limestone foundation - which lays along in horizontal flakes and can be easily broken up for fensing or any other use. The whole country is covered with fine luxuriant grass which supercedes the underwood throughout the Forrest, and their cattle shew the good effects of it. I never have seen such in any Country. It is common for a cow to grow to the size of our oxen and to give 12 Quarts at one milking. Some give that 3 times a day - the oxen are proportionably large and elegantly formed. It really is a pleasure to look at them, they are so fat and sleek. The mutton is fat and well flavoured; but little or no pains is taken with sheep. They seem to be insensible to their value - living here, before the war, and even now, a little removed from the army, is extremely low - 25 cents for a meal and 5 cents for lodging — $1.50 per week for board. I will not at this time enter into a description of that beautiful, highly cultivated and fertile country bordering on the Mohawk River from Schenectady to Utica a distance of 100 miles. It is settled by the Dutch principally, in farms of from 50 to 200 acres.

Whenever I undertake to describe its beauties and the fine effect of this Lake when it first opens to your view from a mountain 12 or 15 miles off from which you gradually descend to its margin - I feel an inclination to become a poet.

The scenery is romantick and beautiful beyond description. The Islands in this Lake, (7 and 8 miles square some of them) are extremely fertile but almost uninhabited. I have almost determined to risque a speculation in some of them. They are, or rather might be made, perfect paradices, and will at some future day be immensely valuable. Towns are now growing up where forests were standing ten years ago. We have game of every kind - Deer, Bear, Pidgeons in thousands. Ducks were very plenty before the war, in summer season, but our Cannon have driven them off to the other Lakes. We get the finest fish by only sending after them - the Black Bass - large pike - perch and salmon; indeed

---

[81] The USS *Constellation*, 38, Captain Thomas Truxton, captured the French frigate *L'Insurgente*, 40, Captain M. P. Barreaut, after a battle on 9 February 1799, the first victory over an enemy warship by a U. S. Navy ship. Midshipman Arthur Sinclair was serving aboard the *Constellation* at the time.

almost every fresh water fish there is. If it were not for the extreme cold of their winters, I should like to bring on a few friends to form a society and settle on one of those rich Islands - giving up the "world its pomp and honors all" and insulating ourselves for ever.

To change the subject - Genl Lewis[82] arrived here two days ago. Some of his aids are acquainted with our friend Sam Archer[83] - they left him not long ago at Niagara. They say he is well and speak highly of him as an officer. He commanded one of the Batteries, which did great execution in the Late battle above.[84] You will no doubt hear from him soon.

You will see that my ship is called after the late gallant General Pike.[85] Her launch excited great interest in this quarter - men, women and children came from *afar* to see it. It was a very beautiful one. I can give you some idea of her. She is 3 feet longer and 1 _ wider than the *Essex* pierced with 28 ports, tons near 1000 and is a most beautiful ship - what an elegant command on the attack. She has a poop[86] and Topgallant - Forecastle[87] as far as the foremast forward and mizen mast aft, and only wants it continued on and bulwarks above to make such a ship as the *Constellation*.

You may wish to know the state of our army here. There are about 3000 effective men - but they really make me sick at the stomache to look at them. They remind me very much of the water street Hogs of Norfolk well fed and lazy and muddy as the devil. Really I never saw such looking troops in any Country. Figure to yourself the dirtiest and most slovenly looking blackguards you every have seen, and you have our army, generally, in your own minds eye. The fittest of the army, *if they have any*, is the worst in the world. I believe the men are brave but they want officers and discipline. They fill our ships full of vermin whenever they act as transports for them.

They are little better than savages in battle. Forsyths Riflemen[88] who have distinguished themselves in all the actions. Shoot the Officers, and as soon as

---

[82] Major General Morgan Lewis (1754-1844) had begun the war as the quartermaster general, but was moved to an active station in the spring of 1813. During Dearborn's illness in June Lewis assumed command of the army on the Niagara Peninsula.

[83] Captain Samuel Archer of the 2nd U.S. Artillery Regiment.

[84] The American attack on Fort George, 27 May 1813.

[85] Brigadier General Zebulon Pike (1779-1813) led the American attack force landed at York on 27 April 1813 and was killed during the battle.

[86] The poop was a deck built above the quarterdeck, allowing for the construction of accomodations at the rear of the quarterdeck and used as an additional gun platform.

[87] A topgallant forecastle was a deck built above the forecastle.

"Her launch excited great interest in this quarter..."

they fall they do not stop to load again before they run up and plunder his Epauletts, watch - &c. Some of them have had handkerchiefs full, and have made several hundred dollars in one battle. They have mashed up, between two stones, some of the most elegant Silver embost urns, turines and plate of every discription to get them in their napsacks. The officers, generally attempt to prevent it; but Forsyth is a perfect savage himself. He it is said encourages it. He is as brave a brute as any in the woods. A number of aneckdotes are told of him. Some person killed a favourite sergeant of his, for which he singled out two of the enemy, by pointing first at one and then at another [telling] one of his men to "shoot that fellow - thats the one who shot the Sergeant. Not him that is the one," and so he goes on as fast as one is shot (for those fellows seldom miss) he finds out another. I am told that hundreds have [been] found shot between the pit of the Stomach and forehead - never but by a Rifle. He never obeys orders, yet he has turned the fate of the battle several times.

We have heard by our officer who arrived here last Night that Norfolk[89] has been attacked, and that the enemy were defeated with great slaughter. God send it may be true. I have not received a letter from my dear Sally[90] for a fortnight and only one since my arrival - that was from Richmond. They were all well then - numbers of letters miscarry to this place. I have no doubt but she has written me frequently. I got a letter from George[91] the other day, who had arrived in Richmond to escort her to Mecklinburg[92] to Erasmus'[93] and before this she arrived in her old neighbourhood for the first time since our marriage. I wish you had have written me how Mrs. Robinson was.[94] I have been anxious to hear of her better health. Offer to your wife and family the affectionate regards of your friend.

        A. Sinclair

N. B. Give me a letter just as long as this and as soon as possible.

---

[88] Major Benjamin Forsyth of the U.S. Rifle Regiment.

[89] On 25 June 1813, the British launched a raid against Norfolk, Virginia. It was sent from Admiral John Borlase Warren's fleet off the Chesapeake Bay under the command of Rear Admiral George Cockburn and succeeded in capturing and holding Norfolk for ten days. Provisions were seized and American batteries destroyed.

[90] Sarah "Sally" Skipwith (Kennon) Sinclair (1791-1827).

[91] George Kennon, youngest brother of Sally Sinclair.

[92] Mecklenburg County, Virginia.

[93] Erasmus Kennon, younger brother of Sally Sinclair.

[94] Mrs. Robinson. There is insufficient information available to identify this woman.

**Sackets Harbor - On bd the U. S. Ship *Gen'l Pike*
August the 25th, 1813**

My Dear Jack

Have received your *communication* from *camp*, dated the 10 Inst, I was not, as you seemed to calculate I would be, much *surprized* at finding you had taken the field. As I well knew your zeal for the cause, and when the Enemy invaded our native soil I would have been much surprized at any young Virginian who would remain quietly at his home.

Since I wrote you last we have been out and have met the Enemy, but without any thing decisive having taken place;[95] for instead of finding Sir James Yeo that desperate hot headed boy which report has made him appear, we found him a judicious cautious and skillful commander. Fortune never favoured a man more than he was favoured. Were there not a thousand to attest the fact I should be loth to assert it where I was not known. We have, in the course of the week or ten days which we were in sight of each other, gained the wind on him seven different times, by manoeuvring, and as often lost it by sudden and unexpected changes when we have been nearly within gunshot, and sometimes when we have exchanged broadsides; which at once placed it in his power to give or refuse us Battle; and as the weather was smooth and such as placed it in the power of our Schooner Gunboats to act effectively on him, he studiously avoided it. He has decidedly the advantage by having 34 guns[96] more mounted that we have, and those consentrated in six regular built vessels of war,[97] all sailing alike and able to support each other in any weather - capable of keeping the sea and acting efficiently when our Gunboats dare not cast their guns loose. He has come out upon us with a large new Brig[98] we knew nothing of until she was nearly ready, and it seems they have dismantled a number of sloops of war at Quebec, and are bringing up their men and materials, and that

---

[95] It was not until 7 August that the two squadrons encountered each other. During the next five days they manoeuvred around each other at the western end of the lake, until they broke off contact on the 12th. They were in sight again on the 16th and 17th, but nothing was accomplished.

[96] Sinclair's comparison of ordnance is inaccurate. According to reports that the commodores compiled about their own squadrons prior to the first encounters of the two squadrons, the British mounted 78 carronades and 19 long guns (total - 97), while the Americans mounted 46 carronades and 70 long guns (total - 116). Due to the sinking of two American schooners and the capture of two others, 24 guns were lost by the time of Sinclair's letter.

[97] Although Commodore Yeo had many complaints about the vessels built for the Provincial Marine, it appears that his experienced Royal Navy officers and men were able to handle them with impressive precision through the summer meetings of the squadrons.

[98] The *Lord Melville*, 14, launched at Point Frederick in July 1813.

a builder with 250 carpenters has arrived, under contract to build a vessel of 20 guns every 40 days.[99] All this they can well do, you know as they do not regard expense. I wrote Mr. Munford[100] a detailed account of a particular action we had had, and requested him to let you know the particulars. It was in a letter to my wife, enclosed to him, as I had time only to write her.

We came in for provisions - arrived at 12 o'clock[101] and sailed again at 12 at night. We are now in, having followed the Enemy down the Lake to Kingston. I hope our army will exert themselves to take that place before they increase their Naval force. That, and Montreal is the *Root* at which the *Axe* should have been first directed cut off the communication from their resources, and the upper provinces must fall of course, instead of which they have began at the wrong end, for were they to beat them at the upper end of the province and continue to drive them down, unless there was a force in their rear, they would be like a snow ball, daily accumulating as they rolled back upon themselves.

I presume, before this reaches you, that Comdr Chauncey's official letter will have been made publick and you will there see a detailed account of our cruize. I never pittyed a man more in my life that I do him.[102] He is a brave enterprising man but has had rather too high an opinion of those confounded gunboats,[103] which he now finds of very little service, as they are a mere drag upon the ships, and until we can choose our own time, by having light winds and the weather gage, they will count without being at all usefull. We have them constantly in tow, and as soon as cast off they drift out of the line.

I am quite mortified at the horrid licensiousness of some of our prints. I read the British account of our skirmish with Sir James, extracted into the

---

[99] This information was false. The building of an additional ship had been discussed, but no project was underway at Point Frederick at this date.

[100] William Munford was Sally Sinclair's uncle, brother of her mother, Elizabeth Beverley (Munford) Kennon.

[101] 13 August 1813.

[102] For a discussion of Chauncey's management of the Lake Ontario campaigns, see Robert Malcomson, "Commodore Isaac Chauncey: No 'Average' Officer," *Naval History*, in print.

[103] The squadron that Commodore Chauncey led onto the lake in April 1813 included as many as eleven schooners, which had been merchant vessels prior to having been purchased into the navy and converted to serve as gunboats. These vessels had been built with shallow draughts so that they could pass over the sand bars that covered most harbors around the lake. When the schooners were armed with heavy ordnance, munitions and large crews, they became "top heavy" and were very unwieldy when the wind rose. While deeper and purpose-built vessels like the *Pike* could sail in a relatively true line, the schooner/gunboats were often blown out of line and could not carry heavy spreads of canvas for fear of being upset.

Ogdensburg Paper. It is, as usual, an egregious falsehood - scarsely a word of truth in it. It states our refusing him battle repeatedly, and in the night actions of the 10th where he took two of our Schooners,[104] by their disobeying their orders and running into his mouth, he accuses us of running so fast he could not come up with us - when, the fact was, he had the weather gage and as soon as he got abreast of this ship and she opened upon him he put his helm down[105] and braced sharp upon a wind, while I made two tacks[106] to try and gain his wake that we might save those two imprudent men in the Schooners. It was our wish, oweing to his compact force being more managible than ours, to avoid a night action. But when we saw him coming down we edged off a little, formed our schooners in a line to windward of us, with orders to gall the van Ship all they could, and as they were prest to retreat under our lee, while our two Ships and the *Oneida* formed a close line of cover for them. They all obeyed except the two which in their zeal to injure the enemy, and believing he would not attend to them but come down and give us battles, tacked and got right in his way and were taken, without its being in our power to relieve them. They fought, as the enemy acknowledge, their two ships & the Brig, 20 minutes, and were within half pistol shot[107] before they surrendered.

The Flag,[108] we have had over, expresses great respect for a fierce [?][109] defence, and thought with us, until they got on board them, that they might have [?] cleared their decks - but they killed only one man having cut them altogether in the rigging - while those poor little vessels did *them* much more injury. We lost two of our Strongest schooners,[110] by their upseting in the night

---

[104] The US Schooners *Julia*, 2, Sailing Master James Trant, and *Growler*, 5, Lieutenant David Deacon, were captured by Commodore Yeo's squadron around midnight on 10 August after the two commanders failed to follow the instructions of Commodore Chauncey. This event occurred as the British chased the Americans with Chauncey attempting to lure Yeo closer to his guns.

[105] The manoeuvre, helm down, required the ship's wheel to be turned toward the wind so the ship could tack.

[106] A ship tacked when it turned so that its bow passed through the eye of the wind.

[107] Half pistol shot was a distance of about 25 feet.

[108] Under a flag of truce, a vessel was sent from Kingston to Sackets to deliver a letter from Yeo to Chauncey regarding the capture and the prisoners. "Flags" frequently traveled between ports.

[109] Due to damage to the original document, identification of the exact word preceding these brackets is unclear.

[110] The schooners *Hamilton*, 9, Lieutenant Walter Winter, and *Scourge*, 10, Sailing Master Joseph Osgood, were upset in a storm early on the morning of 8 August 1813 as they lay among the American squadron about 7 miles north of present day St. Catharines, Ontario.

in a Squall. They had 19 guns & 70 men between them, only twelve were saved, and those by other vessels accidentally running on them, as we, not being at all distrest by the wind in this Ship, did not even suspect they had upset until late in the morning; but as we had been carrying hard sail all night to try and weather the Enemy, we supposed they had drifted out of sight.

This inhuman Monster of an Editor, remarks at the bottom of his publication - after exulting in our losses, that those two vessels in carrying sail *to get away from the Enemy* had upset and drowned 100 men - "and supposing themselves insufficient to act above water had gone down to try their skill as Torpedoes, and that we might soon expect to learn they blown the *Wolfe* up &ct."

What does such fellows deserve? Hanging is too good for them. We have built, out of the remaining timber of this Ship,[111] a vessel of 340 Tons, and she is now rigged and ready to receive her armament, for which she is waiting; and you will be astonished when I tell you she is a beautiful vessel and her keel was only laid the 25th day of last month. As we have not others, we are going to lay up some of the gunboats and put four of the heavy guns on her. This will enable us to bring one more in the line in any weather. And I trust in god that altho they are superior we shall be able to beat them yet.

Do you know Colnl Cocke that you should never address an officer under his grade, and that I have been a Master Commander for more than a year and am now a Post Captain, the highest grade in our Navy and you are addressing me by the old fashioned title of Lieut Comdr. If you don't address me respectfully I won't call you Colnl that I won't.[112]

A sloop of war being, now, below my grade and particularly as the Comdr has changed his pendant to this ship, I am in hourly expectation of being ordered to the command of one of the new Frigates. We must be very tenacious of this sort of right for if a Post Captain is once kept in a Sloop, it may be sited as a precedent and all may be made to feet it. I am sure I deserve a long letter in reply to this. Offer my love to your wife and children, if not in person, do so when you write. Oh! how I want to see mine. I have been but a few weeks with

---

[111] The US Schooner *Sylph* was designed by Henry Eckford and launched at Sackets Harbor on 18 August. Its dimensions are unknown, but it was pierced for 18 guns, which made the British assume when they first viewed the schooner that a significant increase in ordnance had been made by the Americans. At first, however, the vessel was armed with four, 32-pounder long guns, mounted on pivots. By the spring of 1814, it was altered into a brig and armed with eighteen, 24-pounder carronades.

[112] A long list of naval promotions, dated 24 July, was approved by Congress on 2 August 1813. Among them was Sinclair's advancement to the rank of captain. As the next letter in this series shows, Sinclair had never been satisfied with the arrangement aboard the *Pike*, and his promotion made his situation even less desirable.

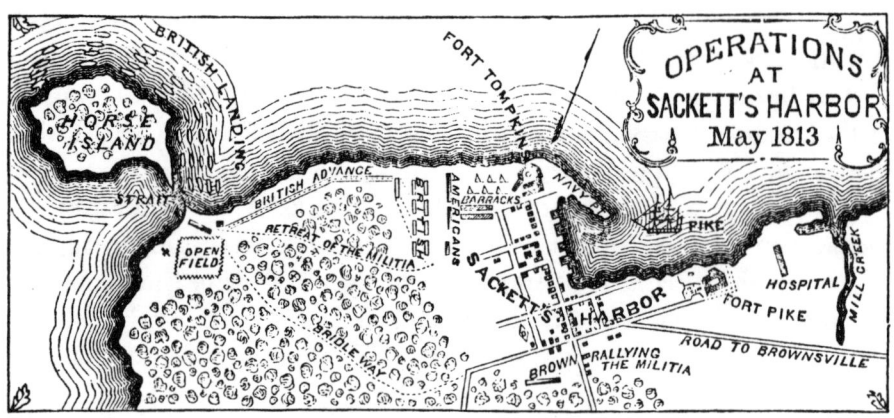

Operations at Sackets Harbor, May 1813.
From Benjamin J. Lossing's *Pictorial Field-book of the War of 1812.*

Commodore Isaac CHAUNCEY
United States Navy

them for near 18 months. I am sure we ought to be well rewarded for such privations.

Wilkinson[113] arrived here two days since.

Your friend
A. Sinclair

• • • • • • • • •

United States Ship *Genl Pike* - Sackets Harbor
August the 22 - 1813

Sir:[114]

When you ordered me on the Lake service, and to take the command of the finest ship of my grade, I received the order as complimentary and obeyed it with alacrity, but on my arrival here I was much disappointed and mortified to find that the Comdr intended shifting his Flag onto her and that I was, consequently, to lose the command of *the ship* which had been held out to me as an inducement to leave the Atlantick. However, being in a *particular manner* ordered, by you, to this ship, and believing that it was not contemplated by you to place me in an undesirable situation, I gave up all personal consideration and determined to suffer any privation rather than risque its being thought that I considered individual right more than the good of the service in which I was engaged. I therefore remained without even communicating to you my feelings on the subject.

Altho the office of Comdrs Captain would not be voluntarily held by the *junior master commandant* in the navy on the *first class ship* in the service, it being but a small remove, in the estimation of our officers, from that of a 1st Lieut, and as to any honor the ship may gain, his participation in it is no more than any other subaltern.

The rank which the government has now done me this honor to confer upon me, has placed it out of my power, with anything like justice to myself or respect for the grade I hold, to remain longer in this situation, without making known to you my sentiments on the subject, and requesting you to place me in one such

---

[113] Major General James Wilkinson (1757-1825) took charge of the U. S. Army situated on the northern border east of Lake Erie after Henry Dearborn's retirement in July 1813.

[114] This letter diverges from the Cocke correspondence by being addressed to William Jones (1760-1831), Secretary of the Navy between January 1813 and December 1814. It is Sinclair's formal request for assignment to a station more appropriate to his rank of captain and is included in "Letters received by the Secretary of the Navy: Captains' Letters, 1805-1861", USNA, RG 45, 1813, vol. 30, Microcopy 125, Reel 30, item 140.

"... I have the greatest confidence in him as an officer."

as you may think consistent with my rank, and such as well place it out of the power of those of the same grade with myself to think I am doing an injustice to their standing. In the mean time, until I can hear from you, altho my present situation affords no chance for personal fame, in the combat which must shortly take place, I shall remain where I am and use all the means in my power to insure it to my country.

I am confident, *you* will not for a moment, think that I am dissatisfied upon any other score than a sense of right, but to prevent an improper construction being placed on it, by those who are unacquainted [?] with service, I think it proper to state that I have not only a personal regard for the Commander in chief here, but I have the greatest confidence in him as an officer and there is none in the service under whom I would more willingly serve.

I have the honor to remain, Sir,
with great respect your Obt [obedient] Servant
A. Sinclair

· · · · · · · · · ·

Capt. Arthur Sinclair,
Comg the U. S. Ship *Gen Pike*,   Navy Department
Sackets Harbor.   Septr 16th 1813.[115]

Sir:

I have received your letter of the 22nd *Ult*.[116] and as the circumstances, of which you complain, have arisen out of that of your promotion, and the nature of the service in which that promotion found you, I think your view of the case, has rendered it more irksome than its real merits warrant.

The *Gen Pike* is, in all respects, a Captain's Command, and it is very natural for the Commodore to hoist his Pendant on board the best ship in the fleet.

As to the terms, or inducements, you intimate to have been held out to you, in the *particular manner* in which you were ordered to the *Gen Pike*, it must be the result of your own imagination. I thought it as high a command as you had a right to expect, and higher than you had in view, when you wished to decline that of the *Argus*, for one of the new sloops of war.[117] I have yet to learn that

---

[115] The source of this letter is "Letters Sent by the Secretary of the Navy to Officers, 1798-1868," USNA, RG 45, Microcopy 149, Reel 11, item 90.

[116] *Ultimo* means "last", as in "the 22nd last" (month).

[117] In January 1813 Congress approved the building of three large frigates and six sloops. Two of the sloops, the *Erie* and *Ontario*, were built along the lines of the *Argus* at Baltimore. They were launched before the war was over, but due to the British blockade did not see any action.

officers have a right to select the service of the Atlantic, or the Lakes or that any inducement is necessary, but that of an order from the Department to proceed on any service.

If promotion was to render necessary the instantaneous abandonment of an important service, in which the officer might be engaged, because he conceived his new rank to entitle him to a higher command, the Government might find it necessary to postpone that preferment, lest the service should suffer by the sudden transfer at a critical moment.

If it is true, that the "Office of Commodore's Captain would not be voluntarily held by the junior Master Commandant in the Navy," I can only say, that the pretensions of Officers are extravagant, and unwarrantable, and entirely unsupported by the practice of the Navy, for you know, that a Commodore, on the Mediterranean service, has had a *Captain* in the Navy.

At present there is no suitable command for you elsewhere. When such a command shall occur you will be gratified, and if, in receipt of this, you shall find your present situation so irksome, as to render a state of inactivity more desirable than a continuance until the close of the season, I will immediately order an officer to relieve you.

I am, respectfully,
your Obedient Servt.
W. Jones[118]

· · · · · · · · ·

United States Ship *Genl Pike* - Sackets Harbor
October the 10th, 1813

I have not heard from you, my dear Jack, for a long time, neither have I written to you, as I have been so much occupied of late that I have scarsely had time to write even to my wife.

Since the 30th of July when we first sailed we have merely put into port for a few hours, in order to fill up our stores; sometimes we come in at night - work all night, and out in the morning. The service all together is the most unpleasant and laborious, you can imagine. The enemies fleet, sailing in Squadron, is infinitely superior to ours; they can therefore avoid an action all most when they

---

[118] Jones's comments helped Sinclair to resign himself to his situation. He did not reply to Jones, although he brought up the matter again when he next wrote to Cocke. Sinclair left Sackets for medical reasons in December, but reluctantly returned to the lakes in 1814 as commodore of the Lake Erie squadron. The highest ranking subordinate officer on his flagship was a lieutenant.

please, and as Sir James has wished to keep up the appearance of commanding the Lake he has kept out and harrassed us by continually tantalizing us with battle (by keeping us in sight) and refusing always to meet us. By this means we are almost worn out with fatigue at Quarters. Sometimes we know not what sleep is for a week at a time except what we can nod about the decks, continually laying our guns. I had rather serve 12 months on the Ocean than 3 on the Lakes - the fatigue would be less.[119]

We have had three encounters with him. The one on the 10th of August at night I believe I have given you an account of - he got two of our small schooners by their Commanders using more bravery than prudence and disobeying their orders. He was to windward of us, and they tacked without orders and suffered him to get between us and them. We have however paid him for it in our last cruize. We have taken the same two back, with three others, burned one and run a seventh on shore. We got with them, too, about two hundred and fifty of the flower of their army belonging to the Baron De Watteville Legion[120] - among them were two field officers. They are the finest looking men I have ever seen, and it appears that they have held out the idea to those men that they must never surrender as not Quarters were ever shewn by the Americans. The poor devils trembled like criminals when they came onboard, but as soon as they found a treatment so different (for you know a german Soldier is the merest slave on earth) they wished to join our service. I think when those men return and acquaint their companions of their treatment, that the whole of them will desert. It is well known too that they are much dissatisfied with the treatment of the English.

---

[119] The depth of this comparison was great, especially in light of an endurance test Sinclair had survived before coming to Lake Ontario. Between 23 December 1812 and 17 January 1813 the US Brig *Nautilus*, under command of Sinclair, then a master commandant, had been buffeted by a series of tremendous gales that led to its partial dismasting, cutting away of its guns and injury to its officers and crew. Their survival was considered a miracle. Sinclair's first lieutenant at the time was Walter Winter (later the ill-fated commander of the schooner *Hamilton*), who pressed charges against Sinclair for his conduct during the storms. After a court martial, the charges were dismissed. See McKee, *A Gentlemanly and Honourable Profession* ... pp. 138-146.

[120] On 5 October Chauncey's squadron sighted, south of the Prince Edward Peninsula, and chased a supply convoy of 7 British vessels sailing for Kingston. The Americans succeeded in capturing the schooners *Confiance* (ex- *Julia*), *Hamilton* (ex-*Growler*), *Mary Ann* and *Lady Gore* and the cutter *Drummond*. The sloop *Betsy* was burned by the British, and the schooner *Enterprise* escaped to Kingston. Among the 152 British prisoners were 82 officers and men of De Watteville's Regiment, a foreign corps shipped from Spain to Quebec during the spring of 1813. This event, and the previous capture of the American schooners, featuring accounts by Wingfield and Myers, is the topic of Robert Malcomson, "The Captures of the schooner *Julia/Confiance*," *American Neptune*, 51 (1991), pp. 83-90.

"We had warm work of it..."

You have no doubt heard much of Sir James Yeo's vaunting after he took those two schooners, saying we had lost two others, upset in trying to get off from him &c. When we were in Niagara in the fore part of September, we were windbound for several days - during which time he paraded before the mouth of the River as if he was blockading us. This was done in face of both armies. However on the 7th of the month the wind changed and we went out. He lay with his Topsails aback in line of Battle, colours flying and great shew of bravery. I thought he was going to fight us like a man and prepared to meet him; but as we drew near he began to edge off and we had the satisfaction of chasing him all round the head of the Lake for three days in front of both armies where all could judge for themselves.

On the 10th we pushed him so hard that he made down the Lake. We overtook him off Genessee River by his geting becalmed and our bringing the breeze up to him. He had every sail out, and was towing and sweeping to get off.[121] This Ship lead the van[122] and was the only one which got in good striking distance. We had warm work of it for between five and six hours and had our Schooners done their duty we must have had him. The time was calm and smooth and just suited for them; but they are commanded by a set of boys without the least experience or judgment. The Ship *Madison* and Brig *Oneida* having carronades were of no service. My ship was much cut in sails and rigging and six or seven shot in the hull - only one man slightly wounded - and we were the only one touched. He was very much cut as we could then see and have since learned.[123] Sam Archer was with me a volunteer, with a mortar mounted on one of the 24pdr carriages on the T. G. Forecastle. He threw some good shells out, she dismounted herself the 12th shot, and I hoisted the 24 pdr in her place and gave him the command of her. He is a fine brave officer and I am pleased to hear, stands very high in the army.

When we had chased Sir James into Kingston we proceded to Niagara to convoy our troops[124] down to this place where they are to form a junction, and it is said to strike a blow, at this late period, where they ought to have done it

---

[121] Sweeps were long oars, usually passed through specially cut ports, that were each manned by a number of men who then rowed the vessel, not unlike an ancient row galley. This exhausting procedure was conducted in hope of bringing the vessel to a place where a breath of wind might stir the sails.

[122] The "van" was the lead position in a line of ships.

[123] Commodore Yeo reported a midshipman and four others killed and six wounded and more damage to the *Royal George* and *Melville* than the other vessels.

[124] A brigade of 3,000 Americans was assembled by Major General Wilkinson at Niagara for transportation to Sackets Harbor. They would form part of the army that would begin a campaign on the St. Lawrence River.

at first - that is, somewhere about the *Root*. We had been there a day or two, when we learned he had sneaked up to the Head of the Lake and was watching our motions, with an intention to attack us when full of Troops, and lumbered. We went out on the 27th - on the 28th found him over towards York. We fortunately had the wind from the eastward, and him under our lee so that by running he must alternately bring up at the head of the Bay.[125] He run entirely across the Lake in trying to get the wind of us,[126] and got so far a head of us that when he tacked he headed for this ship who was in the van. He set his colours and when he got oposite, his whole line opened upon us.

He no doubt expected that we should pass broadsides with him[127] and by tacking astern of him, he would lead us another dance across the Lake and by that means bring on night or gain the wind of us and get off. In this he was disappointed for instead of tacking I wore[128] this ship right oposite him and, covering our whole fleet run right down for him disregarding his fire, until within good distance when I hauled up[129] and opened an elegant fire on him. The first broadside made him bear away two points[130] and make the signal for his fleet to make more sail, in ten minutes for the time I commenced my fire he was a wreck. His main and mizen topmasts with the yards topgallant masts and all their appendages were down among his guns.[131] He kept off right before the wind - which was his only alternative, for you know a Ship sails nearly as fast in that way with one mast as with all.[132] He was elegantly covered by the

---

[125] Chauncey's squadron approached Yeo's squadron from the east with the wind at its back, thereby having attained the wind gauge.

[126] Yeo's squadron sailed southward at right angles to the Americans.

[127] Sinclair speculates that Yeo expected the Americans to return his fire immediately by changing course slightly to the southwest, so that the two lines of warships would pass each other, exchanging their broadsides. Chauncey did not order this movement. Instead, he maintained a straight line, at near right angles, for the British, steering to engage the *Wolfe* at the van of the British line.

[128] To wear a ship, the vessel was turned so that its stern passed through the eye of the wind.

[129] When he deemed the distance was close enough for his broadsides to be effective, Commodore Chauncey probably asked Sinclair to turn the *Pike* so that its guns could bear on the *Wolfe*.

[130] There are 32 points in the compass, so the movement of the *Wolfe* involved a slight veering away from the *Pike*.

[131] The main topmast of the *Wolfe* collapsed onto the deck, carrying with it the mizen topmast. Probably, this accident was caused by the cutting of the stays, or heavy rigging that supported the main topmast.

[132] Commodore Yeo ordered the *Wolfe* to be turned so that the wind was directly astern, by which means the sails on the foremast could be used to propel the ship. This was a difficult manoeuvre »»

Royal George[133] and his other vessels, all of whom aimed at this ship to disable her. In this way we made a running fight of it for three hours (this ship alone getting into action) which brought us near the head of the Bay.[134]

This was the most trying time I ever had in my life.[135] The wind was blowing a gale right into this narrow bay full forty miles deep, owned on all sides by the enemy, the weather showing every appearance of the Equinoctial gale, and their whole fleet so completely disabled that they must either go on shore or surrender in less than an hour if we dare persue them; but the calculation was, we must all go on home together, and altho we conquered them, yet we should be their prisoners, as they were covered by their army with a quantity of artillery. And should any vessel be saved she would be theirs and give them the command of the Lakes. This determined the Commodore to haul off and give up the victory.[136] The *Royal George* lost her Fore topmast also, the moment she came by the wind to anchor.[137] We were prevented from seeing this by her being head on to us (we have since heard it) otherwise we might have gone in with safety, as this Ship, the *Madison*, *Oneida* Brig, and *Sylph* could have gone in and both their heavy vessels were complete defenceless, the probability was, that we would be so disabled by the others, as to prevent our beating out after forsing them on shore.

»» owing to the wreckage on deck and hanging over the side of the vessel, which was still under fire from the Americans.

[133] From his position as second in line behind the *Wolfe*, Commander William Mulcaster moved the *Royal George* ahead to intercede between the *Pike* and the damaged flagship, a manoeuvre greatly praised by all who saw it.

[134] This engagement became known as the "Burlington Races" since both squadrons raced westward toward Burlington Bay before a rising wind out of the east, which at the time was the name given to the body of water on the lake side of the extensive sand bar that enclosed what was then called the Little Lake.

[135] For a discussion of the September actions, see Thomas Malcomson, "September 1813: The Decisively Indecisive Engagements between Chauncey and Yeo," *Inland Seas*, 47 (1991), pp. 299-313.

[136] The Americans turned away from the British because they feared that they would be trapped in Burlington Bay by the strong eastern gale and possibly cast upon the enemy's shore by the storm.

[137] The *Royal George* lost a topgallant mast as it anchored. The British squadron came to anchor at a holding ground on the lake shore east of the narrow and shallow channel that cut through the sand bar into Little Lake. A popular, but untrue, story is that the squadron passed through the sand bar into Little Lake, which was impossible given the nature of the channel, the size of the vessels and the severity of the weather.

[138] Chauncey's commodore's pennant flew from the peak of the main mast, and the commodore's presence inhibited Sinclair's desire for independence.

"We were unfortunate in one of our guns bursting..."

How unfortunate it is that I have the Flag[138] onboard my ship, I should have done quite as much, and indeed more, without it, as I could have turned my attention to smaller objects, in the capture of some of their smaller vessels. I once cut of the *Prince Regent*[139] - and had the *Melville* Brig under my guns, both of which I could have captured by bearing the fire of the *Royal George* a few minutes unreturned. One of those vessels saw us sheer once to give a broadside to the ship, and thinking it was for her she hauled her colours nearly down, but hoisted them again, past my Bows in the smoke and got down to her line. Here we might have got 30 guns from the Enemy, which added to us would have made 60 difference. We could have laid up all our gunboats, and kept the command of the Lakes as completely as if we had destroyed them all.

I beged the Comdr to let me take them, but he was so sure of all, he *exclaimed all or none*. I am clear for every advantage which offers being improved in detail. Thus you see with what this Ship has done, and would have done. Had she not borne the Flag I might have, as a Captain, immortalized myself; but now, altho she whipped the whole Fleet, *it may be considered* she has done no more than her duty. See what we suffered - the ship, until we stopt the shot holes would scarcely float, her fore, mainmast & Bowsprit wounded and Rigging and Sails cut all to pieces 27 men Killed and wounded, and the other vessels scaresly touched and not a man hurt. We were unfortunate in one of our guns bursting which made great slaughter. It killed men on the Quarter deck although it bursted on the Forecastle. Our guns cast to the Eastward are horrid things. Several others of them are cracked, and we find them filled up with lead where they have been flawed. Such are yankee tricks.

Our Navy still proves successful. The Affair of Perrys on the other Lake is unequaled.[140] The *Enterprise* and *Boxer* is a brilliant affair[141] - and the *Argus* and *Garland*[142] still more so.

---

[139] The schooner had been renamed the *General Beresford* during the previous May.

[140] Perry's Lake Erie squadron captured all six vessels in the British squadron after a fierce three hour engagement near Put-in-Bay on 10 September 1813.

[141] The US Brig *Enterprise*, 16, Lieutenant William Burrows, captured HM Brig *Boxer*, 14, Lieutenant Samuel Blythe, after a 30 minute battle off Portland, Maine on 5 September 1813. Both commanders were killed in the action.

[142] Sinclair must be referring to the engagement between the US Brig *Argus*, 16, Lieutenant William Henry Allen and HM Brig *Pelican*, 18, Commander John F. Maples, off the coast of Ireland on 14 August 1813. The British captured the American brig, and Allen suffered a mortal wound.

[143] As master commandant of the *Argus*, Sinclair made an independent cruise on the Atlantic between mid-October 1812 and early January 1813. He captured a few insignificant British merchant ships and eluded a British squadron that pursued him for three days.

Does it not appear hard that I cruized all over the Ocean in the latter vessel[143] for six months of the war, fell in with nothing but line of Battle Ships and Frigates, was chased almost to death, nearly starved - and most of my prizes recaptured, and those that have come in turned out badly; and Allen, only in a trip to France has immortalized himself?

The Rank I now hold in service entitles me to a *Frigate* and *nothing less*, but I will even suffer this degradation of remaining as I am, until we either destroy the enemy or exhaust the Season. My creed is, that the first consideration of an officer should be the good of his country - secondly his own rights, and I shall act agreeable to it. I hope to have a little leisure time after this campaign. If I have, I will come up and spend a few tranquil weeks with my old and valued friend, free from the toils and hardships of war.

Offer my affectionate regards to your Nancy[144] and all the household, and believe me most truly your friend.

A. Sinclair

NB I was told just now by Capt Crane,[145] of the *Madison*, that I had a high compliment paid me by the Commodore in a few words - "That I was a brave and gallant seaman and he was much indebted to me for the masterly stile in which I handled my ship in all the actions & that I had enemies, but they were envious ones." I am sure this will please my friend and to such only would I mention it, another might think it vanity. I have visited the grandest sight in nature - the Falls of Niagara. I must defer any discription until we meet and then I shall be able to do but little justice to their magnificence.

· · · · · · · · ·

United States Ship *Genl Pike*, Sackets Harbor
November the 30th, 1813

It is with unspeakable regret, my old friend, that I have it not in my power to announce to you what your letter of the 8th Inst[146] appeared to anticipate, and what I confidently believed myself would have been the case before the close of this campaign, that is the capture of Kingston and distruction of Sir James' Fleet.

---

[144] Insufficient information is available to identify this woman. Nancy may have been the nickname for Cocke's wife, Ann Blaus (Barraud) Cocke.

[145] Master Commandant William Crane (1784-1846) was sent to Sackets Harbor during the late spring of 1813.

[146] *Instant* means "current," as in "the 8th of the current month."

I have no language to express the mortification of our brave commander and all the officers (I may say too, the crews) of our Squadron, as it was a matter perfectly understood that we were to be seconded by the army, which was all that was necessary to have insured us success the most complete. I am mortified more for my Country than individually so, as I feel confident of having done my duty to the utmost of my power, and I am as certain that had the ample means furnished by the government been properly applied she would have had no excuse to regret the want of reputation.

It is scarsely necessary to recapitulate to you, who are in the habit of reading the papers, that we have been pioneers for the army upon both Lakes this whole campaign.[147] The capture of York, of Fort George, Malden, the destruction of Procter's Army,[148] the transportation of two armies from the Head of the Lake to this place without the loss of a single Boat, has been effected by the aid of the Navy; and see the return they have made us at the close of the campaign. After driving Sir James from the Lake, capturing a part of the force which was to have been employed against our Army, and convoying them safely to this place, a council of war was held, in which the Navy participated and Kingston was agreed upon to be the point of attack - in favour of which decision there were many forcible reasons. First that as their grand arsonal and depo, where they were building three large ships,[149] one of which is calculated to carry 64 guns, and if not distroyed must necessarily oblige our country to build an equal force at a vast expense, and to answer but a temporary purpose. Secondly it was unmilitary to leave an army of 3 or 4000 men in their rear in possession of so strong a hold. Thirdly it would have saved the necessity of an Army here this winter, merely for the protection of the navy which when the ice sets in must always be exposed to a superior force garrison only 30 miles from it. It is also as perfect a key to the upper province when in possession of the strongest naval force, as Montreal can be. A landing could have been made too, above and below Kingston which would have insured the surrender of the force there to our Army, which was double its strength, and of course able to divide in that way.

---

[147] For a discussion of navy/army relations, see William S. Dudley, "Commodore Isaac Chauncey and U. S. Joint Operations on Lake Ontario, 1813-14", *New Interpretations in Naval History,* Cogar, pp. 139-155.

[148] After his victory at Put-in-Bay, Oliver Hazard Perry's squadron transported Major General William Henry Harrison's army to invade southwestern Upper Canada and subsequently defeat the British army under Major General Henry Procter at Moraviantown on 5 October 1813.

[149] By this date the two British ships that would be launched the following April, HMS *Prince Regent, 56,* and HMS *Princess Charlotte, 40,* were under construction at Point Frederick.

Under a firm belief that this was a fixed plan, we sailed to Blockade Kingston, and after an unaccountable delay of near three weeks, at this late season, they assembled at the mouth of the St. Lawrence where we met them in full hopes of an attack the next day.[150] When to our unspeakable mortification we were told that they had given up the plan, and were about to descend the St. Lawrence to Montreal. This could not be effected without our aid; but we were to participate only in the risque - and this no small one - to descend a rappid River in the face of a superior force, at a season when we were in daily expectation of the ice setting in, strong westerly winds prevailing, every point capable of being fortified by the Enemy and our pilots ignorant of the navigation except for craft.[151]

However we were determined that nothing on our part should be wanting to further their views whither we approved or disapproved of their movements. We therefore descended the River to the lower end of Long Island, a point where the Enemies channel comes into ours and forms the main body of the River. Here we were met by Sir James, who was hastening down to distroy our Boats, but anchored the instant he saw us.[152] The pass between us and him was narrow, difficult and just the depth of water through, which this ship drew. He had the wind favourable for him to pass, and laid nearly within gunshot of us until it changed in our favour to pass to him, which we were about venturing when he got underway and made the best of his way back for Kingston.

The Indian Summer now set in and we remained here a week of as fine weather as I ever saw, confidently believing the two armies had united and were

---

[150] Major General Wilkinson had assembled an army numbering nearly 8,000 men at Sackets and had begun moving them to Grenadier Island in stages in preparation for a descent upon the British. Kingston had long been identified as the target, but deliberations between Wilkinson and Secretary of War John Armstrong led to Montreal being selected around 20 October as the target. Chauncey, whose vessels had helped to transport the army and cover their movements, was not informed of the change of plan until 29 October. The commodore was dismayed by the alteration and opposed to the new plan.

[151] Wilkinson wanted Chauncey's squadron to accompany his flotilla of boats as far down the St. Lawrence River as possible. Chauncey limited his assistance, fearing that Yeo's squadron would blockade the mouth of the river, trapping the Americans who would soon be caught in ice and vulnerable to military attack.

[152] On 5 November 1813 the American squadron was anchored in the St. Lawrence River at the eastern end of Wolfe Island (referred to here by Sinclair as Long Island) when all six of Yeo's vessels sailed down the Kingston Channel and anchored five miles away near the foot of the island. A string of islands and shoals separated the two squadrons. Chauncey ordered a channel to be found and buoyed and the *Pike* and *Sylph* to be lightened so that their long guns might be brought into range of the enemy. On the morning of 6 November Yeo withdrew, whereupon Chauncey ordered the return upriver to the lake.

in possession of their object - Montreal. The sad reverse of which and all their movements you are before this time acquainted.[153] Genl Wilkinson informed us that the Secretary of War overruled him, and altered the premediated attack on Kingston. If so I should not be astonished to find, that he has an object in view, which I will state to you when we meet.

The St. Lawrence is one of the most noble and beautiful Rivers in the world, and will in time float the greater part of the produce of our country to a market. The navigation of the rapids which was once thought impossible, are now, you see navigated by *armies* in safety. The innumerable Islands in this River are fertile and beautiful beyond description. They abound with Deer and game of every kind but are as yet uninhabited.

Carlton Island which contains about four or five square miles of high land, and is one of the richest spots I ever was on, is situated just within the entrance of the channel on our side and is the Gibraltar of that pass. In its west end there is one of the most regular forts[154] in our country. This Island was seded to us by treaty in 83, in which agreement it appears we were to pay for the Fort; but they valued it at £80,000 sterling, a price our government thought extravagant which has kept it ever since in dispute. It is on the south of both channels and must of course be ours. At the commencement of the war they burned the Barracks and abandoned the Fort. Here it was we feared that Sir James Yeo would come round to, moor his fleet and fortify. In which event we should have been forced to run the gauntlet the Kingston channel. The Deer of this Island are innumerable, it is finely timbered and the grass generally knee high and as green now under the snow, as it was two months ago. What a desirable spot this for a farmer to settle with a stock of marino sheep, and a breed of cattle from this country which are full as large again as ours.

On our arrival from this expedition with an intention of laying up, finding the Enemy has done so, the Comdr received a letter from the Secretary of War saying that unless we transported Harrisons[155] army from Fort George, we should be without protection this winter. I believe he thought it impossible on account of the season; but wished to *shark* himself out of the scrape his management had brought us in. The wind was fine from the East. We immediately sailed and fortunately arrived and embarked the troops the third

---

[153] After landing on the British side of the St. Lawrence River, a portion of Wilkinson's army was beaten by a smaller British force under Lieutenant Colonel Joseph Morrison at the Battle of Crysler's Farm on 11 November 1813. Wilkinson withdrew his force to the American side of the river and gave up his campaign against Montreal.

[154] Fort Carleton.

[155] Major General William Henry Harrison (1773-1841).

"*Many of them had men washed overboard ...*"

day after.[156] It then increased to a dreadful snow storm and blew from that point for 3 days - separated our fleet, did a considerable damage and had it blown 24 hours longer the Enemies shore must have brought up a majority of them. Some of them lost masts - some sails, some rudders in attempting shallow harbours.[157] Many of them had men washed overboard; but we have at last all arrived here. The troops suffered much, but I met no accident in this ship.

Genl Harrison came down with me, and finding him a Virginian and from our old neighbourhood, I could not but feel an extraordinary interest for him. I gave him my Bed, which he kept very closely the whole passage. I found him a brother of Carter B. Harrison. He is a plane, unaffected, intelligent man. Most of his aids are Virginians or Kentuckyans originally from Virginia. Separating and coming in singly as we have, is a strong evidence, if further evidence is wanting, that we have command of the Lake.

We have just received information by the *Lady of the Lake*[158] who has been over as a Flag to Sir James - that he was dangerously wounded in the action of the 28th Septr. by a 24 pdr shot from this ship. It carried off a large part of the flesh from one of his thighs and he just now begins to hobble upon crutches.[159] He acknowledges his being whiped that day - that the fighting was over, and his trains were already laid for blowing his ships up after running on shore, if fortune had not favoured him with the weather it did - and further states that we were indebted to this ship for the whole victory. A victory it certainly was to all intents and purposes - and deserves much more credit than the state of the publick mind at that time prompted them to give us. Perry's victory could not be rivaled, and anything short of it disappointed the publick. On what a slender thread does expectation hang - by a soldier - hard to be gained - difficult to be kept, and easy to be lost.

We also learn that had we attacked Kingston but little resistance would have been made. They had a Council a few days before our army descended the River determined to abandon that with the upper province, and burn their fleet both

---

[156] The squadron departed from the Niagara River on 16 November.

[157] The schooner *Governor Tompkins* lost its rudder going over the bar to anchor in the Niagara River. The schooner *Fair American* ran ashore attempting the same thing. The *Julia* almost went ashore at Burlington.

[158] The schooner *Lady of the Lake* was built by Henry Eckford at Sackets Harbor during the winter of 1813 and launched on 6 April. Often compared to speedy pilot boats at New York, information is lacking about its dimensions other than its burthen, which was recorded as 89 tons.

[159] No evidence has been found to confirm this story about Commodore Yeo being wounded.

building and on float. The passing of that place has been most fatal to the campaign and will run our country to incalculable expense.

You were right in your expectations that I would not leave the station during the campaign altho my situation here was below my Rank. I felt it a duty I owed those of my grade to state this to the government; but at the same time volunteered to remain the season unless we got possession of the Enemy sooner. The Secretary has promised my return as soon as we lay up, and the first command he can give me.

I am now detained as president of a court martial on Capt Leonard of the Navy,[160] which I fear will be a tedious one. I never was more anxious to see or hear from my family. The 20th of last month was my last letter from them. I am quite uneasy at not hearing since, the mails here are very uncertain. Yours of the 8th only arrived yesterday. I have been but a few weeks with my family for the last two years, and but very little since I was a married man. I think I deserve a little indulgence now. If I get it I will come and see you; but if there is service for me I will not ask it during the war.

Hi Ho! how much more hard cruizing and d____d hard fighting have we had than many who have received publick thanks[161] - freedom of the citys in gold Boxes - swords and dinners and lord knows what - and here we may travel home - without the *freedom of all cities to pass through them unnoticed - pay for our own dinners* and not a Box to take a chew or a pinch out of, or a sword to kill Sir James when we come within striking distance of him - and all because he has had the heel [?][162] of us.

Offer my love to your wife, children, and all the family and believe me yours affectionately and truly.

A. Sinclair

NB - I will let you know in my next where to write to me which I hope you will not delay to do. One of our *Honorable fraternity*, a spy has this moment arrived from Kingston, and brings us information that Sir G Prevost is collecting all his forces to attack Wilkinson. I fear for the result. If Hampton[163] does not join

---

[160] Master Commandant James Leonard was tried before a court martial convened aboard the *Pike* between 1 and 9 December on charges of neglect of duty and conduct unbefitting an officer. He was found guilty and was ultimately suspended from the service for one year.

[161] Naval officers like Perry, Isaac Hull, Stephen Decatur and others had been rewarded generously for their victories over the British.

[162] Although Sinclair's script is unclear at this point of his letter, he appears to be referring to the British having escaped by sailing away from the Americans and turning the "heel," or the point at which the sternpost meets the keel, to them.

[163] Major General Wade Hampton (1751 or 52 -1835) had led an army from Lake Champlain to join Wilkinson's army in an attack upon Montreal. His march was stopped by a defeat at the »»

him and still refuses, or has, as is said, already refused to do so I trust in god a court will hang him. No private peak should operate upon the duty of a soldier.

The large ship[164] of the Enemy is planked up and the other two geting on fast. Saml Archer is with Wilkinson. I left him well. If your letter to him is in this post office I will try and forward it.

HMS Prince Regent *1814*

»» Battle of Chateauguay, 25 October 1813, and no meeting with Wilkinson was achieved. The objectives of the campaign were also impeded by poor personal relations between the two generals.

164 This was probably HMS *Prince Regent*. Only one other ship, the *Princess Charlotte*, was under construction.

Lieutenant Henry KENT
Royal Navy

III.
The Narrative of Lieutenant Henry Kent
Royal Navy

1814

Kingston, on Lake Ontario, June 20th, 1814

1. Setting Out on the Journey

We left Halifax in the *Fantome*,[165] on the 22d of January last, and arrived at Saint John (New Brunswick), on the 26th, making a passage of four days, the weather extremely bad; the brig appeared a complete mass of ice, it freezing as fast as the sea broke over us. The inhabitants of Saint John came forward in the most handsome manner in a subscription to forward us in sleighs to Fredericton, the seat of government, a distance of 80 miles. The seamen were divided into three divisions, each of 70 men, the first under Captain Collier[166] of the *Manly*, the second under Lieutenant Russell,[167] and the third under myself. On the 29th of January the first division proceeded about nine in the morning, and in the afternoon the second followed; the next morning I disembarked, the rigging of all the ships being manned, and the crews cheering us.

On landing, we were received by the band of the 8th regiment,[168] and a large concourse of people, who escorted us to the sleighs, when we set off at full speed. In eight hours we went fifty miles, and then halted for the night at a small

---

[165] HM Sloop *Fantome*, 18, Commander John Lawrence, who had help to capture the brig from the French in 1810.

[166] Commander Edward Collier (1783-1859?) entered the Royal Navy in 1796. He was advanced to lieutenant in 1803 and commander in 1810. In January 1813 he volunteered, to Rear Admiral Edward Griffith (commanding at Halifax), the 60-man crew of his brig *Manly*, 14, for service on the Great Lakes. Griffith placed Collier in charge of a detachment of 210 officers and men drawn from the *Manly*, the brig *Thistle*, 12, and the sloops *Fantome* and *Arab*, 18.

[167] Lieutenant William Russell, RN.

[168] The second battalion of the 8th Regiment soon left Saint John to take the overland route to Quebec.

"... the brig appeared a complete mass of ice."

house on the banks of the river; started again in the morning, and in the afternoon reached Fredericton, and found both divisions had halted there. The seamen were lodged in a barrack, which was walled in, but they soon scaled the walls, and were running about the town; you may therefore judge what trouble we had to collect them again. The seamen were now divided into two divisions, the first under Captain Collier's command, the second under mine, as being the senior officer.

2. Through the Wintry Drifts

On the 2d of February, Captain Collier proceeded with his division in sleighs, furnished by the inhabitants at their own expense, and the day following I left with mine: I was obliged to leave one of my best seamen sick at the hospital, frost bitten, and I have since learnt that he lost two of his toes. From Fredericton we continued on the ice of the River Saint John, except in places where, from shoals, the ice is thrown up in heaps. The country, after leaving Fredericton, is but thinly inhabited; a settlement you may see occasionally, but never more than three houses together. I kept always in the wake of the first division, halting where they had the day before. On the third evening, at the house where I halted, I found the master of the *Thistle* a corpse,[169] having died with intense cold. Captain Collier having made every arrangement for burying him, I put his body into a sleigh, and sent it to a village a few miles distant.

On the 7th reached Presque Isle, where there is a barrack and depôt for provisions, but no houses near it; this place is 82 miles from Fredericton. Discharged the sleighs, and began making preparations for our march, each of us being furnished with a pair of snow shoes, two pair of moccasans, a toboggin between every four men, a camp kettle to every twelve, with axes and tinder-box.

As you may not know the use of those articles by their Indian names, I will endeavour to describe them: Snow shoes are of a singular shape, something like a pear, formed by a loop, and the bottom of them netted across with the hide of some animal; they are fixed by a strap round the heel, and tied across the instep, as you do a pair of skates; they are about two feet in length, and one in breadth. Moccasans are made of buffalo's hide, sole and tops in one, roughly sewed up with twine, a strip of hide run through notches, cut round the quarters, to haul it tight on your foot. Toboggins are hand sleighs, about four feet in length, and one in breadth, made of such light wood that they do not

---

[169] The master was the only man to die during the expedition. Nineteen others were injured and three deserted.

"... *their treading the snow down which made a small path just sufficient for one man to walk on.*"

weigh above four pounds. On these you lash your provisions and clothes, and with the bight of a rope over your shoulder, drag it with great ease on the snow.

I provided myself at Halifax with a jacket, trowsers, and waistcoat, lined with fine flannel, so that with those, three flannel shirts, and a linen one, three pair of stockings, and a square piece of blanket wrapped on my feet, with moccasans over all, I felt pretty warm.

At day-break, commenced lashing our provisions on the toboggins, and at eight o'clock commenced our march. The clothes I had with me being four shirts, the same of stockings, a coat and trowsers, with a great coat, and a cap to sleep in. We marched daily for fifteen to twenty-two miles, and though that appears but a little distance, yet, with the snow up to our knees, was as much as any man could do. The first night we reached two small huts, the next, the same accommodation, and the third slept in the woods. On the fourth, reached the Grand Falls, which are about forty feet in height; none of us saw them, as they were a mile distant, and all of us too fatigued to go that distance: next day reached a small French settlement on Grande Riviere.

The march from here to Madawaska (another French settlement), was beyond any thing you can conceive; it blew a gale of wind from the northward, and the drift of snow was so great, it was almost impossible to discern a man a hundred yards distant: before I got half way, the men lay down, saying they could not possibly go further; I endeavoured by every persuasion to cheer them, and succeeded in getting about one half to accompany me. We reached it about nine o'clock at night, almost fainting, a distance of 21 miles, The following morning, having sent all the midshipmen in search of the men; I was therefore obliged to halt for a day to recruit them. The next morning, being the 15th of February, renewed our march, leaving a midshipman and 10 men behind sick, chiefly frost bitten.

The three following nights slept in the woods, after going each day about 15 miles on the River Madawaska, where, finding the ice in many places broken through, I made the men take the banks of the river, but continued on the ice all the way myself. On the 18th, crossed the Lake Temiscouata: it was here we were apprehensive of being cut off by the enemy, being in the territory of the United States; however we did not fall in with them. On the 19th, commenced our march across the Grande Portage, or neck of land between the above Lake and the River St. Lawrence; this was dreadfully fatiguing, continually marching up and down hill, and the snow upwards of five feet deep.

The other division being ahead, was very serviceable to us by their treading the snow down, which made a small path just sufficient for one man to walk on, but frequently, in slipping our feet off the path, we went up to our shoulders in snow; got half way through this night, and again deep in the woods: the distance through in 38 miles.

3. On to Quebec

On the afternoon of the 20th reached the St. Lawrence, and found thirty carioles[170] waiting to convey us to the Riviere de Caps,[171] a French village about three miles distant. The next day procured carioles for all the men to Kamouraska, another village 15 miles distant. On the 22d reached Riviere Ouelle,[172] a neat little village, distant from Kamouraska about 12 miles. I should mention, that from Kamouraska to Kingston is 478 miles, which we were obliged to march, as on our arrival at Quebec we had not sufficient interest to procure more sleighs than sufficient to carry our provisions, baggage and sick. On the 24th reached St. Rocques, another village, distant 13 miles; the 25th, La Porte, 15 miles; the 26th, St. Thomas, 18 miles; the 27th, Berthier, 10 miles; and on the 28th, Point Levis, opposite Quebec, a distance of 20 miles.

On the following morning launched the canoes through the broken ice, and crossed over to the city. You would have been much diverted to see the Canadians in the canoes, watching a favourable opportunity to get through the ice, and perhaps each taking a different route; some got entangled, and were not able to extricate themselves for hours; at the same time drifting up and down as the current set them. In attempting to launch one over the ice, I fell through up to my neck, and was two hours before I could get my clothes shifted.

Marched the people on board the *Æolus*[173] and *Indian*[174], lying in Wolf's Cove, and then gave them leave to go on shore. The following morning the first division again proceeded on the march, and the next morning myself, with the second followed. I forgot mentioning to you an unfortunate accident which happened to me on the second day of our march from Presque Isle: by a severe fall on the ice, I broke the bone of the fore finger of my right hand, between the knuckle and the wrist, so that for five weeks I had my hand in splints, and suspended in a sling, which I found not a little inconvenience from, and not until my arrival here did the bone unite, and then so awkwardly as to leave a very considerable lump on my hand; I have lost the use of my knuckle, but can use the finger, as you may see by my writing.

---

[170] Sleighs.

[171] At, or near, Rivière-du-Loup, Quebec. From here to the city of Quebec the divisions proceeded along the main road on the south side of the St. Lawrence River.

[172] Rivière Ouelle, Quebec.

[173] HMS *Æolus*, 32, was sailed to Canada by Captain Stephen Popham who left it at Quebec to go with his crew to join Yeo's squadron at Kingston.

[174] HM Sloop *Indian*, 18, had also been laid up at Quebec while its crew was sent to Kingston.

4. From Quebec to Kingston

The first day of our march from Quebec, stopped for the night at Saint-Augustin, 15 miles distant from that city. On the 3d, at Cape Sante, 15 miles. On the 4th, at Grondines, 18 miles. On the 5th, at Baptisca, 10 miles. On the 6th, arrived at Trois Rivieres, 21 miles; this is considered the third river in Canada. I did not halt here, but marched three miles beyond it, to avoid the trouble of collecting the people, as I knew they were too tired to walk back that distance. On the 7th, stopped at Machiche, 15 miles. On the 8th, at Maskinonge, 16 miles. On the 9th, at Berthier, 17 miles. On the 19th, at La Valtre, 15 miles. On the 11th, at Reperrigue, 15 miles; and the early morning marched through Montreal to Lachine, 12 miles beyond it. On passing the monument erected to the memory of the immortal Lord Nelson,[175] halted, and gave three cheers, which much pleased the inhabitants.

From Montreal to this place we were eleven days performing a journey of 190 miles; the places where we stopped I have not noted, as we seldom found a village, but mostly scattered houses, inhabited by all nations; *viz*, English, Scotch, Dutch, American, and few French. We passed several tremendous Rapids; the Long Sault in particular, which was most awfully grand to look at. We likewise passed Crysler's Farm, where Colonel Morrison defeated General Wilkinson's army, with a mere handful of men.

On the 22d of March we reached this place: the officers and seamen of the squadron were drawn out to receive us with three cheers: we were lodged in a block-house, and allowed four days to recruit. I was then appointed to the gun-boat service (as was Lieutenant Russell), under Captain Owen.[176] In a few days I joined the *Princess Charlotte*,[177] of 42 guns, commanded by Captain William Howe Mulcaster, as first lieutenant. The *Regent*[178] and her were on the stocks, planked up, and their decks laying. The *Regent* is about eight feet longer than our 38-gun frigates, having fifteen ports on each side of her main-deck, and

---

[175] A statue to honour the late naval hero was erected in Montreal in 1808.

[176] Commander Charles Cunliffe Owen mentioned in Part I.

[177] The *Princess Charlotte* was designed by George Record and launched at Point Frederick on 14 April 1814. It was a frigate measuring 126 feet, 9 inches on the gundeck, 37 feet, 4 inches abeam and pierced for 40 guns. It was originally named the *Vitoria*, but this name was changed while the ship was still on the stocks.

[178] The *Prince Regent* referred to here was not the schooner launched in July 1812, but rather a frigate designed by Patrick Fleming and launched at Point Frederick on 14 April 1814. It was 160 feet, 9 inches long on the gundeck, 43 feet abeam and pierced for 56 guns. Being the largest vessel then afloat on Lake Ontario, the *Regent* replaced the *Wolfe* as Commodore Yeo's flagship.

guns on her gangways, so that she carries twenty-eight long 24-pounders on her main-deck; eight 68-pound carronades, two long 18, and eighteen 32-pound carronades on her upper deck, with a complement of 550 men. The *Princess Charlotte* is about the length of a 32-gun frigate, but eighteen inches more beam, pierced for thirteen ports on her main-deck, and carrying twenty-four long 24-pounders on that deck, with two 68-pound carronades, and sixteen 32-pound carronades on her upper deck, and a complement of 330 men. The other ships are the *Wolfe* (now the *Montreal*[179]), a ship corvette of 20 guns, chiefly 32-pound carronades, and 120 men; the *Royal George* (now the *Niagara*), of eighteen guns, 32-pound carronades, with a long 24-pounder on a pivot abaft, as in each of these ships; her complement 120 men. Two brigs, the *Star* and *Charwell*, the former of 14, the latter of 16 guns; the largest 100, the other 90 men. Two schooners, the *Magnet* and *Netley*, of 10 guns each, and 75 men. Ten or twelve gun-boats (none of them covered over), one carrying a long 18-pounder and a 32-pound carronade; the others a 32-pound carronade each. The establishment is for three lieutenants to be on the gunboats service, each to a division of four boats, commanded by midshipmen.

From the time of my joining the *Princess Charlotte* I never quitted the ship or barracks. The interval between her launching, till we went to sea, was but eleven days, three of which were occupied in heaving down the ship, to get the cleats off her bottom.[180] The result of our attack upon the enemy's Fort Oswego[181] you already know.

---

[179] The vessels in Yeo's 1813 squadron were renamed on 1 May 1814. When he arrived at Kingston in May 1813 with his original detachment all the officers and men were listed on one "establishment" rather than opening a separate establishment and its accompanying administrative records, or ship's books, for each vessel. The one establishment system became unwieldy as hundreds of naval reinforcements reached Kingston through 1813 and early 1814, so the Admiralty decreed that each vessel would have its own establishment. All the vessels of 1813 became recognized as belonging officially to the Royal Navy and were renamed so that they would not conflict with other vessels on the Navy's list. The name changes were: *Wolfe - Montreal*; *Royal George - Niagara*; *Melville - Star*; *Moira - Charwell*; *Beresford* (originally the schooner *Prince Regent*) *- Netley*; *Sir Sidney Smith* (originally the schooner *Simcoe*, which had been bought into the service by Yeo in May 1813) - *Magnet*. The *Montreal* and *Niagara* were also re-rated as "post" ships at this time, meaning that officers put in charge of them were automatically advanced to the post captains list.

[180] Just prior to the launch of a vessel, a launching cradle was fastened to the rear portion of its hull to keep it upright as shores were knocked aside during the launch. The cradle was usually attached by means of ropes so that it would float free after launch. Presumably, cleats had been attached to the lower hull of the *Charlotte* for use in fastening the ropes.

[181] The British attack on Oswego on 6 May 1814 is detailed in Section IV, the second part of James Richardson's memoir.

IV.
The Memoirs of
Master James Richardson
Royal Navy

Part Two: 1814 - 1815

1. The Attack on Oswego, 6 May 1814

In the Spring of 1814 word having reached our Commodore Sir James Yeo, that a large number of boats were at the mouth of the Oswego River, laden with cannon and stores for the fitting out of the two frigates then being built at Sackets Harbor, an expedition was ordered for the capture of the fort at that place, now named Fort Ontario,[182] our squadron consisting of the *Prince Regent*, 58 guns; *Princess Charlotte*, 40 guns; *Wolfe*, 20 guns; *Royal George*, 20; *Moira*, 16; *Melville*, 16; and *Netley*, 12; with detachments of troops[183] from the Royals, Glengarry Fencibles and other corps, left Kingston on May 4th and arrived off Oswego on the 5th, but owing to heavy squalls of wind they were obliged to haul off, and delay the attack till next day.

In the morning of the 6th, orders were given for the *Wolfe* (subsequently named the *Montreal*) to stand in and take up position under the fort to cover and assist with the landing of the troops. The charge of conducting her to her anchorage among the rocks and shoals that environ the entrance of that river devolved on me, and not without some degree of diffidence did I perform the

---

[182] Although Commodore Yeo observed in his report about the action that the fort and town were "in point of position ... the most formidable I have seen in Upper Canada (sic)" (Yeo to Croker, 9 May 1814, NAC, MG 12, Admiralty 1, vol. 2737, p. 40), the fort itself comprised three earthern ramparts and a breastwork surrounded by a fosse. Only four long guns were mounted there and the position was defended by about 300 men from the 3rd U. S. Artillery Regiment under the command of Lieutenant Colonel George E. Mitchell. There was no defensive force in the village, located across the bay from the fort.

[183] The brigade embarked in the squadron consisted of 450 men from the De Watteville Regiment, 50 men from the Glengarry Light Infantry Fencible Regiment, 24 Royal Artillerists, Six Rocketeers from the Royal Artillery, 20 Sappers from the Engineer Corps and about 400 Royal Marines from the Second Marine Battalion. Command of the military detachment was in the hands of Lieutenant General Gordon Drummond. See Robert Malcomson, "War on Lake Ontario: A Costly Victory at Oswego, 1814." *The Beaver*, 75 (1995), pp. 4-13.

task; for not since I was a lad had I been there, and then only in small vessels; with very light draught of water.[184]

I resolved, however, on doing my best, though sensible of the weighty responsibility resting on me.

I succeeded in securing the desired position to the satisfaction of both my captain, Stephen Popham[185] and Commodore Yeo, who were pleased to commend my conduct in their official despatches.

Our gunners had a rather warm berth after the gunners of the Fort obtained the range, every shot telling on some part of her, a fixed object at anchor.

The shots which they complimented us were evidently "hot," for they set our ship on fire three times. One of them made so free with me as to carry off my left arm just below the shoulder, which rendered amputation at the shoulder joint necessary.[186] Our position was obtained before the troops were ready to land, the other vessels keeping in the offing, so that we alone for some time had to be under fire from the Fort.

The *Melville* brig and the schooner *Netley* at length came within range of the batteries to our assistance. In the meantime, while the troops with some sailors and marines, having effected a landing, marched directly up the hill, and scaled the fort, under a galling fire from the enemy, which cut down a goodly number of our men, both officers and privates.

Among the wounded was the gallant Captain Mulcaster of the *Princess Charlotte*, who received a musket shot in the abdomen, from which he never fully recovered, though he survived for several years, honoured by the notice and confidence of His Majesty William IV, who placed him on his Staff as aide-de-camp at his Court.[187]

---

[184] Although the bay at Oswego had a wide and deep anchorage, the mouth of the river was often obstructed by a bar after the spring floods had run off. This hazard had prevented Oswego from being chosen as the base for the American squadron, which would have been preferable to Sackets Harbor since it was linked by water to the Mohawk River and the Hudson River. Most heavy ordnance and ship materiel passed through Oswego on their way to Sackets.

[185] Stephen Popham (1780-1842) entered the Royal Navy in 1795. He was advanced to lieutenant in 1801 and to commander in 1811. As captain of HMS *Æolus*, 32, he arrived at Quebec in October 1813 under orders to transfer his crew of 350 officers and men, plus all the fittings they could remove from the ship, to Kingston.

[186] Commodore Yeo noted in his report of the battle: "Captain Popham ... speaks in high terms of Mr. Richardson the Master, who from a severe wound in the left arm was obliged to undergo amputation at the shoulder joint." A footnote in the Richardson memoir adds: "Lieutenant Richardson always maintained that at the moment, in the excitement of the battle, he was unconscious of this; later wishing to use his arm, he found it gone."

[187] Mulcaster's wound was caused by a musket ball that penetrated his body near a groin muscle, too high on the leg to allow for amputation. At first it was thought he would die within hours, but »»

As our forces entered the Fort in front, the enemy abandoned it from the rear, and though the victory was thus gallantly achieved and the Fort reduced, the object sought by the expedition was not obtained. The flotilla of boats laden with arms and stores, above mentioned, being, with the exception of one, ten miles up the river, and beyond our reach, as our force was not sufficient to penetrate the country. Therefore, with the exception of one boat and some other stores which fell in our hands, nothing was gained with the sacrifice.[188]

The Fort, after being reduced and dismantled, was abandoned, our troops retiring at their leisure, not "driven away with loss" as some of the American chronicles have recorded.

2. The Battle of Sandy Creek, 30 May 1814

There is rather a painful sequel to the history of the said flotilla:— Our Commander failing to get them as expected at the mouth of the Oswego River, kept on the watch and blockaded the place for several weeks, so as to nab them on their emerging from the river, well knowing that unless they could get into the lake the cannon and naval stores could not reach the ships at Sackets Harbor, as the roads were unfit for the transport of such large stores. But after the lapse of some months, the vigilance of the blockaders probably having been relaxed, and the Americans being on the alert, they stole a march one foggy night and morning, and got several miles down the coast before being discovered.[189] Captains Popham and Spilsbury[190] with some armed boats[191]

»» he survived and was sent to England to recuperate. Mulcaster later married and fathered four children, but his wound never healed adequately and he suffered tremendously because of it. Just before his death in 1837 he was appointed a naval aid to King William IV. A biographical sketch written about him following his death contains an account of the attack on Oswego and the treatment of his wound. See NAC, MG 24, F 95.

[188] The official British reports of the attack differ in the amount of goods captured, but it appears that three schooners, heavy rigging materials and more than 1000 barrels of salt, tallow and food were seized.

[189] A convoy of 19 bateaux carrying long guns and cables departed from Oswego early on 28 May 1814 under the leadership of Master Commandant Melancthon Woolsey of the U. S. Navy and the protection of Major Daniel Appling and 130 riflemen. A group of Oneida Indians joined them during their passage. On the 29th they landed at Salmon Creek and discovered that one of the bateaux was missing. Fearful that the British would soon be looking for them, Woolsey ordered the remaining boats to advance down the coast to Big Sandy Creek and to travel about two miles up that creek to a landing. The resulting skirmish occurred on 30 May.

[190] Francis Brockell Spilsbury (1784-1830) entered the Royal Navy about 1796. He was advanced to lieutenant in 1805, to commander in 1813 when he came to Canada with Commodore Yeo, and to post captain aboard the *Niagara* in the spring of 1814. As a prisoner of war in Chesire, Massachusetts, Spilsbury encountered William Hamilton Merritt, lately captured at the battle »»

"Not a single soul was visible near them, and it seemed a bon *prize ..."*

being on the look-out intercepted one of the enemy's boats in the fog, and were informed by the prisoners that the others had entered Big Sandy Creek.

The prisoners omitted to inform them that the boats were strongly guarded by a body of riflemen and Oneida Indians. Captain Popham being in command, immediately, with more bravery than prudence, pushed in after them, and after penetrating the creek between high banks of sandy marsh on either side, after proceeding about two miles, discovered the boats snugly moored with their precious cargoes, in a kind of basin formed by a bend in the creek. Not a soul was visible near them, and it seemed a *bon* prize, but alas! just as they were grasping them, up started, from their concealment in the woods and rushes, the riflemen and Indians who opened a murderous fire on our poor fellows, cooped up like ducks in a pond.

The result was the destruction or capture of the whole body, not one escaping. Those who survived were kept prisoners of war until peace was proclaimed the ensuing Spring. Lieut. Rose[192] now residing near Cobourg,[193] must be conversant with the incident, as he was one of the captured. I think it was fortunate for me, that my wound still laid me up in sick quarters, for had I been fit for duty, I would in all probability have been ordered to accompany my captain - Captain Popham - on this fatal expedition....

3. The Great Ships of Lake Ontario

[As mentioned above] in the Spring of 1814, there were launched and fitted out from the Kingston dockyard, the *Prince Regent*, a fine ship of 58 guns,

---

»» of Lundy's Lane. Merritt described the captain as: "a blunt, good natured sailor, full of life and action, and can endure any hardship." See W. H. Merritt, "Journal of Events Principally on the Detroit and Niagara Frontiers," in William Wood, ed., *Select British Documents of the Canadian War of 1812* (Toronto, 1928), vol. 3, p. 640.

[191] Popham and Spilsbury led about 200 sailors and Royal Marines in three gun boats and four ship's boats. One hundred seventy-five of the men were taken as prisoners of war. Commodore Yeo was angered greatly by the loss of so many officers and men, especially since he had warned Popham about proceeding into unfamiliar places in search of the enemy.

[192] Likely Lieutenant James Rowe who entered the Royal Navy in 1805, came to Canada with Commodore Yeo and was advanced to lieutenant during the spring of 1814. William Hamilton Merritt said of him: "Rowe almost made his escape near Sandy Creek; he had all his boat's crew killed or wounded, and himself on the point of losing his scalp, an Indian had hold of his hair, when an officer saved him. He is a small, good looking young man, quick tempered, high spirited, very liberal and good hearted."

[193] Following the war Francis Spilsbury returned to settle in Upper Canada. He eventually developed a farm named Osmondthorpe Hall near Cobourg where he was an influential citizen and where other half-pay officers settled, one of which was, presumably, James Rowe.

"The St. Lawrence ... *cost the British nation ... upwards of £800,000 sterling."*

and the *Princess Charlotte* of 40. These were followed on the part of the Americans, by the *Superior*[194] and the *Mohawk*,[195] of force to match the two last mentioned on our part. This led to the building at Kingston of the *St. Lawrence*,[196] mounting 102 guns, and with draught of water of 23 feet.[197] The *St. Lawrence* took the lake in October 1814, and made two trips, up and down, previous to the setting in of Winter, without a chance to try her prowess with the enemy, as he very prudently kept himself close in harbour, so that at the end of the season, which terminated the war, our proud ship and squadron had the lake wholly to themselves.

But, although the fighting terminated, the ship-building did not, for the British Admiralty were so considerate as to frame in the English dockyards, and to forward the frames (perhaps deeming ship timber, a rare material in Canada) two frigates[198] of 36 guns each, one of which, the *Psyché*[199] was sent to Kingston, set up, furnished and fitted up in the Spring of 1815, besides two

---

[194] The USS *Superior* was built by Henry Eckford and launched at Sackets Harbor on 1 May 1814. Details about its dimensions are unknown, but it was designed to rival Yeo's *Prince Regent* by carrying sixty-two guns.

[195] The USS *Mohawk* was built by Henry Eckford and launched at Sackets Harbor on 11 June 1814, only 34 days after its keel was laid. Details about its dimensions are unknown, but Commodore Chauncey compared the ship to the frigate *New York*, which was 144 feet long on the gundeck and 37 feet abeam. The ship had a battery of 42 guns, making it a perfect opponent for Yeo's *Princess Charlotte*.

[196] HMS *St. Lawrence* was designed by William Bell and launched at Point Frederick on 10 September 1814. It was 196 feet, 2 inches long on the gundeck, 52 feet, 7 inches abeam and pierced for 102 guns. This first rate ship was the largest armed sailing ship to ever cruise the lakes. See Robert Malcomson, "HMS *St. Lawrence*: Commodore Yeo's Unique First-Rate," *Freshwater*, 6 (1991), pp. 27-36.

[197] The loaded draught at the stern of the *St. Lawrence* was given as 20 feet. During one of its supply missions to the Niagara Peninsula it was loaded until its draught was 21 feet. Commodore Yeo prevented the loading of other provisions, which he calculated would increase the depth of water to 23 feet.

[198] In January 1814 the Admiralty approved the construction at Chatham dockyard of components for two frigates of 36 guns each, the *Prompté* and the *Psyché*, and two brigs of 18 guns, the *Goshawk* and *Colibri*. Rigging, ordnance, officers and crews were assembled and despatched from England in March. They began reaching Montreal in late May, from where the components for one frigate were painstakingly transported to Kingston through the summer.

[199] HMS *Psyché* was launched at Point Frederick on 25 December 1814. It was 130 feet long on the gundeck, 36 feet, 7 inches abeam. An upper deck was added to the original design so that the ship could be pierced for 56 guns. The ship was rigged in the spring of 1815 and made at least one brief voyage. See Thomas Malcomson, "HMS *Psyché*: A Frigate in Frame," *Seaways' Ships in Scale*, 4 (1993), pp. 16-21.

other large ships,[200] 120 each, which were framed and partly planked during the Summer and afterwards left to rot on the stocks. The ships that were afloat also rotted in Navy Bay, and were sold under the hammer when they were condemned.

The *St. Lawrence*, which when she first sailed out, with her complement of men, arms stores and provisions for one month cost the British nation, as I heard from our purser, upwards of £800,000 sterling, was sold, as I was informed, in her dismantled and condemned condition, under the hammer about the year 1826, for twenty pounds.[201]

Our neighbours, not to be outdone in the race for ships, set up two ships[202] in their dockyards of 120 guns each, which were unfinished at the close of the war, but they took the precaution to build sheds so as to enclose them from the weather, which, I am told, has preserved them to the present time. . . .

When the large ship, the *St. Lawrence* with 23 feet draught, was fitted out, I, having just recovered from the loss of my arm, waited on Commodore Yeo, and reported myself ready for service, he pleasantly remarked: "What, try them again?" I replied, "If my services were required". He exclaimed, "That is noble", and then proposed that, instead of joining my own ship, the *Wolfe*, [*Montreal*] he would prefer taking me in the *St. Lawrence* to aid in piloting her, inasmuch as her draught of water so far exceeded any former vessel on the lake and it would, therefore, require the more caution and matured knowledge of the channel to conduct her safely.

He remarked that my severe wound and consequent debility for some time yet precluded the discharge of my regular active duties in my own ship, but if I gave my services to the *St. Lawrence* as he proposed, he would continue my substitute in the *Wolfe* during the remainder of the season, and that at the close of navigation, I would be at liberty to recruit my strength during the winter. This afforded me an opportunity of acquiring a more thorough knowledge of the depth of water by sounding and exploring unfrequented channels, and...[the

---

[200] Only the frames and some planking were completed on these twin vessels, which were designed by Thomas Strickland and named the *Canada* and *Wolfe*. They were intended to measure 193 feet, 6 inches on the gundeck, 50 feet, 8 inches abeam and pierced for 120 guns.

[201] Having been ordered to sell off the remains of the Lake Ontario squadron, Commodore Robert Barrie, RN, sold the hulk *St. Lawrence* for £25 in January 1832.

[202] The USS *New Orleans* was built by Henry Eckford and Adam and Noah Brown at Sackets Harbor. It was nearly ready for launch when the signing of the Peace of Ghent prompted a shut down. The ship was 212 feet long on the gundeck, 56 feet abeam and intended to carry 120 guns. The ship stood at Sackets until it was demolished in 1883. The second ship was the USS *Chippawa*, either a twin to the *New Orleans* or a 74 gunner measuring 204 feet on the gundeck and 56 feet abeam. It was only partially built at Storrs Harbor, near Sackets, and was demolished in 1824.

water was] as near as I can estimate it has been, on an average, about five feet higher since 1815, than at any time previous in the recollection of the oldest navigator on the Lake.

Action at Oswego, 6 May 1814

Master Barzallai PEASE
United States Army Transport Service

V.

The Journal of Barzallai Pease

United States Army Transport Service

1814

1. A Job in the Transport Service

Early in the spring [of 1814] I engaged to sail a sloop riged scow with leeboard[203] for a Mr. Stiles at Macanack village[204] carrying cotton bales from Hudson[205] to the factory and factory machinery from there to Albany. This was destined for Watertown[206] in Jefferson County. I carried one load to Honburg[207] or rather below, at other times freighting wood. In this way I spent the summer, having only my son Hiram with me, Occationly hiring help to land and unload.

In September I was informed by a friend that the Commander of the United States Transports on Lake Ontario was out of health, and had applyed for his discharg. I obtained a letter of a Gentleman in Hudson to the Quartermaster General[208] to whome I applyed for the office, which he granted me, and on the 6th of the same I was regularly appointed, and with my Warrent Repaired to Sam Brown[209] Sackets Harbor acting Dept. So he put me upon my duty taking

---

[203] This was a one-masted, fore and aft-rigged merchant vessel, not to be confused with a two- or three-masted warship rated as a sloop. Being a scow, this particular vessel had a flat bottom and would drift to leeward as the press of wind increased on the sails. To give the vessel some depth, and grip in the water, a movable keel was attached to either outboard side away from the wind (the leeward side) and lowered into the water.

[204] Possibly, modern-day Mechanicville, 20 miles north of Albany on the Hudson River.

[205] Hudson is located about 30 miles south of Albany on the Hudson River.

[206] Watertown is located about 12 miles east of Sackets Harbor.

[207] Possibly, Hamburg, located about 75 miles south of Albany on the Hudson River.

[208] Elisha Jenkins was appointed the Quartermaster General for the 9th Military District on 22 April 1813. His station was at Albany, New York.

[209] Sam Brown was appointed Deputy Quartermaster General on 26 March 1813.

Captn Robert Mores[210] resignation the Offices whome I superceeded. I was busily engaged in the Charge of the transports which was at this time fiting out upon an expedition, the destination of which I new not, but was in hopes I should now have a chance of seeing something done wherein I should be enabeled to give a good account of my self.

But soon after the Memorable battle on Lake Champlain,[211] General Izards[212] army arived something like five thousand, when he sent for me and wanted to know the state of my fleet, which I gave him a Correct Account. I was then ordered to be in readyness in four days to take the troops on board. I pressed every private vessel, (except one)[213] that would not consent to hire willingly in the Service, and on the day appointed, the Embarkation took place, and in the morning sailed. I went in person, on board the *Julia*.[214] After we started Commodore Chaunceys fleet all sailed haveing the principal part of the troops on board. I was ordered by the Commodore to keep close to his Ship through the day and night, when we lay off and on before the mouth of the Genesee River.

When in the morning,[215] contrary to my calculations, or even wishes we landed all the troops, from whence they marched to Black Rock by land, and the Navy sailed, leaving me to make my own arangments. Some of the transports, I ordered into Oswego after Provisions intending to run in my self but when I arived, saw so bad a sea on the bar I set a signal to bear away from Sackets, and the only one out, schooner *Raven*[216] Wm Coffin[217] bore away

---

[210] Presumably, Mores was the officer whom Pease replaced.

[211] The Battle of Lake Champlain at Plattsburgh, on 11 September 1814, was won by the American squadron, under Master Commandant Thomas Macdonough, which captured most of the British squadron under Captain George Downie.

[212] Major General George Izard (1776-1828) embarked 4300 infantrymen in Chauncey's fleet and the Army transports at Sackets on 21 September 1814 and sailed west to reinforce the American army beseiged at Fort Erie.

[213] An entry in Pease's Journal #15, p. 9 lists eleven vessels and boats belonging to the transport service.

[214] This was the same schooner *Julia* that had been captured by the British on 10 August 1813 and re- captured by the Americans on 5 October 1813. Thereafter it was used expressly as a transport.

[215] 22 September.

[216] Originally, the British merchant schooner *Mary Hatt*, captured by Chauncey's squadron on 10 November 1812 after the *Royal George* had been chased into Kingston.

[217] Insufficient information was found to identify this man further.

following me leaving the *Growler*[218] within the bar at anchor looking very bad. In about five hours we got to Sackets, and in several days all the transports arived, except one which was stranded near Little Sodus.

2. After the War

And thus ended my warlike operations. This place was all in commotion erecting new fortifications planting cannon building ships & boats, with as many malittia as could be necessary were on this post made it appear all in bustle. It being very rainy the mud was half leg deep, which caused the death of many a man at Sackets. In the Month of January, after the Ice had made the vessels useless, I returned to my family on a furlow of sixty days.

About the time I was to leave, Henry Eagle,[219] Agent for Mr. Eckford ship builder New York, offered me the schooner *Julia* and *Growler* for two thousand dollars,[220] but I declined the purchase untill spring, as they would be useless untill that time, when I intended making the purchase. But before my furlow was out we had the news of peace and the *Growler* sold for two thousand five hundred dollars.

This brought to my mind the old proverb, that delays were dangerous, and in fact it proved so in this case to me, at a time when we expected an attack by the enemy, all the woonded and sick, both prisoner and Americans was to be removed to Brownville for safety. I attend the moving them by water as fast as water convayance. Amongst was a man taken as a spie who I believe was to be executed for the same, and to avoid which he abstained from food and when the day arived when he should have been executed he was but just alive, and avoided it but died shortly after. I saw two deserters shot while I was on the station.

On the 15th August 1815 the Transports were sold at public auction. I bid off one called *Raven* at one thousand and seventy dollars. I then applied for my discharge and on the 19th my resignation was accepted, when I took charge of her and sailed her about three months. I then sold out to Christian

---

[218] This was the same schooner *Growler* that had been captured and re-captured along with the *Julia*. It was captured again during the British attack on Oswego on 6 May 1814. Apparently, it later fell back into American hands.

[219] Henry Eagle was a shipwright involved in the building of the *Oneida* and the vessels at Sackets Harbor.

[220] In November 1812 the U. S. Navy purchased the *Julia* for $3800 and the *Growler* (formerly the *Experiment*) for $3200.

"I then applyed for my discharge .... and returned to my family at Hudson."

Sailors of 1812

MEMOIRS AND LETTERS OF NAVAL ... ON ON LAKE ONTARIO

EDITED WITH AN
INTRODUCTION
AND NOTES BY
Bob Malcomson

ILLUSTRATED by George Balbar

"The conflict ahead..." 4th October 1813

ARTHUR SINCLAIR — JAMES RICHARDSON — HENRY KENT — BARZILLAI PEASE

· OLD FORT NIAGARA ASSOCIATION ·

Sailors of 1812

Old Fort Niagara Association

Holmes[221] for the sum of Eighteen hundred Dollars, and returned to my family at Hudson. Here I heard of the loss of my youngest child a son six months old.

This was one of the Errors of my life, if it may be so called, for when I returned to Sackets Harbor in the Spring of 1816, I found business was yet good. And I could not buye another vessel without paying more than I was will to give. The one I had sold was now held at two thousand five hundred dollars, and had the man been willing to part with the whole I think I would have given it. This season I made one trip in the schooner *Wolsey* and then Engaged with the firm of Townsend Bronson[222] &c to sail the schooner *Oswego*, to run as Packet from the Port of Oswego to Niagara, in which I continued untill the season Closed.

During my coasting to the River Niagara I went up to Lewiston where Mr. Townsend resided. I had the privilege of freighting by paying the customary freight. At one time I carryed flour which I sold at Niagara, formerly Newark, and sold to a Raker for three hundred and some odd Dollars. Upwards of A hundred I never have had yet. After my vessel was laid up my owner Mr Bronson offered me the *Niagara Packet* the ensuing season to sail, and would advance my wages ten Dollars per month, but I declined not intending to sail any more on the lake, as I had purchased a farm in the County of Delaware, and my family had moved not during the summer, while I was yet at Oswego on wages.

---

[221] Insufficient information was found to identify this man further.

[222] Townsend was an American merchant who formed a company with Alvin Bronson, usually referred to as Townsend & Bronson. They owned some of the lakers sold to the US Navy at the outset of the war.

About the Editor

Robert Malcomson

Robert Malcomson resides in St. Catharines, Ontario. He is employed as an elementary school teacher in nearby Thorold where he currently teaches history to grade seven and eight students. He is also a freelance writer who specializes in the naval history of the War of 1812. His articles have appeared in numerous magazines, journals and newspapers in Canada and the United States. With his brother, Thomas, he co-wrote *HMS* Detroit: *The Battle for Lake Erie*. He has also written monographs entitled: *The Battle of Queenston Heights, Burying General Brock: The History of Brock's Monuments* and *The Battle of Beaver Dams*. He is currently working on a major study of the naval conflict on Lake Ontario during the 1812 War.

Preserving History At Old Fort Niagara

Since 1927 the preservation and interpretation of Old Fort Niagara have been the goals of the Old Fort Niagara Association, Inc. The Association is a private, not-for-profit organization. Membership is open to anyone with an interest in the Fort and its long history. The Association operates Old Fort Niagara, a State Historic Site, in cooperation with the New York State Office of Parks, Recreation and Historic Preservation.

Old Fort Niagara Publications

Publications are an extension of the Old Fort Niagara Association's educational purpose. Created in 1984, the Publications Committee has been charged with establishing and maintaining an ongoing program of works relevant to the history of Old Fort Niagara. This includes new titles as well as the republication of older works.

Old Fort Niagara Association Publications Committee
Editorial Board:
Harry M. DeBan: Chairman/Publisher
David J. Bertuca; R. Arthur Bowler; Craig O. Burt III; John Burtniak; Richard Cary, Jr.;
Mark Francis; William Lee Nelson-Loefke; Patricia Rice

Additional information about publications, exhibits, programs, or membership in the Old Fort Niagara Association may be obtained from:

Old Fort Niagara
Fort Niagara State Park
P.O. Box 169
Youngstown, New York 14174-0169

• *Sailors of 1812: Memoirs and Letters of Naval Officers on Lake Ontario* •
Production Coordinator, Design and Layout: Harry M. DeBan
Pre-Press: David Bertuca, Harry M. DeBan, James F. Egloff, Robert Malcomson
Production Support: R. Arthur Bowler, Craig O. Burt III, John Burtniak, Richard Cary, Jr.,
Doc D. S. Knight, William Nelson-Loefke and Patricia Rice.
memorare ... Thomas W. Jacobs & A. John Ulrich, United States Navy
Printed in the United States of America on acid-free paper.